**Devantae Butler**

# Mindset

Published by Writers Block Publishing LLC

www.writersblockpublishingllc.com

Booking information for Devantae Butler speaking engagements:

Email: Rndrt.cnp@gmail.com

Instagram: Dare2be_great11

Facebook: Devantae Butler

Subscribe to YouTube channel at RNDRT Reaching New Dreams & Recognizing Talent

**Devantae Butler**

"Do not allow your circumstances to keep you in bondage" – Devantae Butler

# Mindset

© Devantae Butler 2018

www.rndrt.com

Published by Writers Block Publishing LLC.

All rights reserved.

Second Printing.

# Mindset

## Devantae Butler

# Mindset

# **Acknowledgements**

I would like to thank God for the wisdom and guidance to push me to this place where I have found peace and joy in who I am. I would like to thank my parents Demetria Harper and Fred Harper. They have really made an impact on my life through their sacrifices. My siblings Dominick Harper, Dominique Harper, Darius Harper, Demetrious Harper, and Darrell Harper I love them so much. My grandma Darlene Butler and my Aunt Charlene Harper both played important roles in my life and I love them and appreciate them. I would like to say to my family it's an honor to have you guys in my life. Next, I would like to thank my brothers Gregory Deion Coleman, DeJhon Kyles, Tevin Bell, and Michael Roberts for being about this brotherhood, organization, and family (Reaching New Dreams & Recognizing Talents). You guys have kept me motivated and held me accountable and for that brothers; I truly appreciate your sacrifices. There are so many people I can acknowledge right now, and I just want to tell everyone how grateful I am for believing in me. I wrote this book to show others that you can do it too. Not just a book, anything you seek to do. There is no limit to how high you can fly. Just continue to use your wings, and do it through Christ who strengthens you. God is Good, all the time!

**Devantae Butler**

# **Introduction**

I was inspired to write this book to show my generation that dreams really do come true. No matter what you have been through in life, you still have the ability and authority to make positive change. I was not the best student or kid growing up in my neighborhood but more importantly my parents were tough. My biological father wasn't in my life, but God blessed my mom and I with my stepdad, Fred Harper. I believe that everything happens for a reason. Growing up, my stepdad was my best friend. He always treated me like he would his own biological child and taught me lots of great morals. I refer to him as "father," "dad," or simply "my guy." He has truly been one of the greatest additions to my life.

I was never really interested in anything other than football. I studied hard and watched every great player I could find. It showed me a lot about myself. I encourage you to find something you are passionate about, something special to your heart. People may be able to see what's on the outside of you but no one truly knows the size of your heart. I also believe that if you're going to do anything in life you need to do so with love. Love is the most powerful weapon we possess as human beings. Just being kind to someone and saying, "I'm proud of you" can boost their day. Acts of kindness always come back to you. I feel one thing all people need as well is drive. A person needs to be driven when striving for greatness. Greatness isn't temporary, greatness is consistent, so we must identify what we want. We also need vision. I remember as a young kid my mom would say:

"Son, come here."

"Yes Mama?" I would respond.

She would command me to look at my hands and say:

"Son repeat after me, these hands will make me millions."

My Mom was trying to instill a vision in me. We must be able to see our goals and dreams coming true before anyone notices first. Vision is the ability to see further than what is presented in front of you. The only thing I had a vision for was

# Mindset

sports, so this really affected other areas in my life where I was weak. I think that if you're a bad like I was, or not a great student, it's because you truly don't see yourself being a good kid or a better student. The most important thing people need is faith. You cannot always rely on what you know in every moment. Michael Jordan didn't know that he was going to make the game winning basket. He always had a vision to see it first before it happened. He also added faith to the fact that he was going to make the shot. Faith can take you to very high places, but you first must believe when others may doubt you and go against what's in your heart. You must stand strong during this time and allow your opposition to fuel you even more. I feel as if people have a hard time finding acceptance in themselves as well. You must love yourself before you can love someone else, just like you have to see a dream before you can achieve it. These are some key traits that I lacked growing up because I never pressed into them. Even though you are presented with information it does not mean that you know it. We must study this information and learn it before we can present it to others. We must start practicing the information out in our own lives as we are given it. I remember coming home one day and studying the Bible with my mom. She told me something that really stuck with me. She said,

"I am becoming what I read."

I said to myself, that was powerful. Since then, I started training my mind by pouring into it daily to be able to fully understand what she was saying. Now every time I read or I hear information, I listen as if the perspective of this information is for me and only me. It doesn't matter if I'm being directed personally or not. I believe if I hear it or see it, it is for me. I stopped saying what a coincidence to myself and began to say what great purpose. I did the same thing to fix my behavior. I changed my point of view from not blaming other staff members or teaching methods and began to truly put myself in the wrong every time.

Here's the key to the exercise. You must put yourself in the wrong, even when you're right sometimes. I know it's hard to change. That's why it's best to change for the better. I lost

# Devantae Butler

football scholarships because of the characteristics that I maintained since elementary school. I had an elementary mentality in high school because I never took my personal growth seriously. I feel as though you can do anything you put your mind to. The question we must ask ourselves is what are we putting our minds to? What are you invested in the most? For me as a young kid, it was video games. That's all I wanted to do. It was so bad that I would skip homework assignments and studying for mid-term tests, just to play *Madden* or *Call of Duty*. My test scores reflected the work that I was putting in. Therefore, you must really begin to be honest with yourself and set boundaries based on your priorities. Set goals so big that you have to grow into the person who can reach them. Growth is your responsibility and no one else's. Give yourself an assessment on how you are doing daily. It's time to replace our bad habits with good habits. The only way we are going to do that is we must begin to take things seriously. You must decide from the heart that this is what you want. When that happens, nothing will be able to stop you.

Mindset is about how our environment develops our characteristics, that lead to our tendencies as human beings. I want you to know that God is the most important part of my life and He knows what's best for us. I want you to be encouraged. This is your time!

It has been said that, "a mind is a terrible thing to waste," but in many cases as human beings, we do things without thinking about the pros and cons of our actions. In order to take steps to get to another level within ourselves, we must know the difference between being proactive and reactive. Reactive is acting off of impulse, and most of the time, emotion. Proactive is thinking your decision all the way through. The victories of life are in your head and your level of success is determined by the things you tell yourself. Everyone has a choice, however, the differences between most people lie within the decisions made to do something about their circumstances.

Life isn't an easy walk and it cannot be taken lightly. You must feed your mind with the right ingredients to get through.

## Mindset

Every lesson in your life is preparing you to walk into something greater. You must iron out the details with the understanding of what is going on. Praying and asking God for guidance has revealed some things to me and has helped shape me into a better young man. This has been key in exposing me to my weaknesses.

The truth may be the toughest thing to bare as a human, but the quicker you accept it, the faster you can grow. Having the right mindset has taken my life from nothing to something in just a three-year span. I was homeless, broke, unemployed, incarcerated, and suspended from college. These were trying experiences I was forced to learn from and use to build my character. With the Glory of God, I overcame these obstacles and have become an author, motivational speaker, CEO, youth director, and spoken word artist. You too can turn your life around. All you need to do is make a decision. I hope this book helps you gain the tools to take your life to the next level. Just remember, it all starts with your mindset.

**Devantae Butler**

# Chapter One: Why Me?

"Bae, wake Devantae up get him dressed I have to go to class."

I can hear my mother saying when I was five years old. She took me to daycare as she attended college classes during her early twenties. My mother was special, always driven to get things done. She wasn't that fast but was faster than most athletes I know. I grew up in Pittsburgh, PA, in a section known as Homewood. This wasn't the best area to grow up in. I watched struggle take place without knowing the definition of struggle. I loved the game of football and played on a team known as the Baby Twerps, but there was one problem. I was the smallest kid on the team. In fact, I was always the little guy. All my friends and coaches always asked me when I was going to grow. It always stuck with me and I felt like I always had something to prove.

As a kid I was shy because I didn't have a lot. I went to school and I would always get picked on by the other kids who had more than me. Come to find out, the only thing they had that I didn't was confidence. I didn't know how to spell my name until I was ten years old. I always withdrew when it came to knowledge. I always ran away from knowledge because when I got things wrong people would laugh and make fun of me. I didn't want to be wrong anymore. I am the oldest of my siblings, and since I was young, I was told I had to be the example for my sister and brothers. I never expected this role. It was given to me. What challenged me the most was the fact that, in my mind I didn't have anyone I thought of as a role model for me. I just had my parents. The one area I excelled in was the football field, and I was determined to show why I deserved to play. Within football, my dad was my biggest role model and support. He showed me the game and the great players who played. He was the one who had the biggest influence on my mindset.

# Mindset

He always told me:

"Son, it doesn't matter how big they are, because the bigger they are, the harder they fall."

He exposed me to movies like *Rocky*, which is about an underdog boxer who accepted a championship title fight and was expected to lose. That movie showed me the importance of working hard and continuing to fight back. I took what my dad calls a "killer instinct" and began to apply it. I remember when he bought me a Nintendo 64 game system and two games *Mario Cart* and *007*. These two games really helped to shape my character. My dad and I would play together. He was good and he never took it easy on me, and he would beat me every time we played. He also invited more competition over to play, such as my uncle Greg, who would treat me the same way in showing me no mercy. I began to get discouraged and started to play the other game but then I remembered the movie *Rocky* and understood the importance of continuing to fight back. So, I waited for my dad to go to work and I would play all day, every day, until the time came for us to play again. Now my dad was also cocky and he understood his ability, but he overlooked my practice and because of that I beat my dad for the first time! From that point forward, he knew that beating me wouldn't come so easy.

These critical experiences really began to shape my mindset as a young boy. I no longer complained about what I lacked but learned how to work towards what I wanted. I went to football practice the next day ready to outwork every one of my teammates. I knew that on a team of thirty-six kids, I had to stand out. So, I did exactly that. I came in first place every time we ran laps and sprints. I jumped up when coach needed an example, I screamed the loudest, and I learned the most. I didn't have the best talent so I knew I had to mentally equip myself with the knowledge to be successful. I watched great athletes, such as Hines Ward, excel because he was a student of the game. I developed a foundation that stated I can always learn even though I may not be the most gifted. Therefore, I studied the game and other players so that I could be one step ahead of

## Devantae Butler

Everyone else. We must fuel our minds with the proper things so that we can be greater than what is expected from us. These things led me to being named the starting cornerback on my football team unexpectedly. I played great all season and was named defensive player of the year after the season concluded. I never stopped challenging myself to grow and always demanded more by building on the things that I was already doing. Football was my passion and I wanted to become the best athlete possible. As I thought more about it, I noticed that you become what you dwell on. Meaning, when things are happening to you, and you begin to ask yourself *"why me?"* you start to have a complaining mentality that is designed to have you self-destruct. Just begin to look at everything you have complained about throughout the course of your life. I guarantee that there is a higher percentage of the things you have complained about, and you are no longer doing those things anymore. Whether it's a club, organization, or athletic team, when you start complaining about a coach you may not like or a student you don't get along with, you are cheating yourself because you're not 100% engaged. The point is, complaining will keep you frustrated and ultimately prevent you from growing. As much as I complained about my dad beating me at a video game, it only frustrated me more. Now here's the trick, it's ok to be frustrated (we are all human), however, what do you do when you feel frustrated is the question. There are two options: (1) you can either practice to improve, or (2) quit. I'm sure you have heard the saying "quitters never win." Well how true is it really, when you view it from a different perspective? These small examples truly shape and mold us into who we want to be.

Now if you don't like your situation you do have the power to change it by realizing the value of the next moment or opportunity. The answer to "why me?" or "why you?" is what you find after that revelation. Saying to yourself I had to go through this to reach this level in my life. Meaning, what makes you raise your bar and force yourself to push through your feelings or emotions? Adversity? Many people don't like adversity, but great

# Mindset

people love adversity because they love a challenge. If you played any board games against a baby who could barely walk, sooner or later you would get bored and eventually you wouldn't want to play anymore. We all need things that will challenge us so that we stay excited about what we are doing. Adversity breeds greatness! It strengthens you at the same time it tries to get you to quit. We all need adversity to come into our lives to help us raise our bar. Because of my adversity, I can now beat my dad and uncle in anything because even if I lose I know to never quit nor frustrate myself but to get excited and raise my bar. A lot of people are content with where their bar is, but in an affirmation statement it says, "You must give up to go up." So don't be afraid of giving things up because it means you're going up.

    I began to understand the importance of every moment of practice because it truly does make perfect. It will help you take things to that next level. You must approach it like it's your last one every day. Do not complain about what you do not know right away, find the value in the fact that you can grow. Growth is a responsibility, not something that just comes because you are getting older. I was forced to put the work in to see results that I hadn't seen before. How you respond to adversity or challenges will tell you a lot about yourself. It isn't easy to go to practice; it isn't easy to do your homework. The easy route is not doing anything about how you feel or what you want. Marianne Williamson once said, "Our deepest fear is not that we are inadequate. Our deepest fear is that we are powerful beyond measure. It is our light, not our darkness that most frightens us." We cannot continue to run away from how we feel on the inside of us. If you want more, you must believe that you deserve more. Don't settle for what others think about you. Your situation will make you special. When seeking success, you must accept failure. This is difficult but it's worth it at the end. So, stop asking yourself "Why me?" and start saying "Why not me?" You cannot have everything but that doesn't mean you can't grow to be able to give the very things that you wish you would have had to

## Devantae Butler

someone else. Do not get down on your situations, get excited because you can change your circumstance with commitment and determination.

**Mindset**

# Chapter Two: Failure is an option.

Many times we have heard the saying, *failure isn't an option*, however, failure must happen. It is what you do after failing that will indicate if it is a failure or not. At some point in whatever you are doing, you must seek that next level. It is a demand. Whatever it is that you love doing and are passionate about, you must continue to climb that ladder. I believe everyone's ladder steps are different. One of the biggest distractions is focusing on someone else's steps. It is your job to prioritize your goals to come into alignment with your dreams. Mistakes will be made, but we must accept mistakes just as much as we want success. In the same way that you can't have a left hand without a right hand, you can't experience success without mistakes. One hand is more dominant than the other, however, we still must deal with the other hand.

Playing football before my teenage years I knew that school was important but that coaches didn't truly hold players accountable in their academics. I wasn't the best student and during this time, I did only enough to get by. Once I got into middle school, you had to maintain a 2.0 GPA to play sports. I knew that in order to take sports to the next stage I had to be academically equipped to play. I had the wrong thoughts in my head when I was in middle school and high school. I constantly thought about how cool I was, girls, clothes, and shoes. I was worried about being the class clown. I developed the wrong sense of attitude with moving from Homewood to Monroeville, which was a different/better area to live. In Homewood, school work and grades weren't a focus but in Monroeville they were. The students were smart and everyone got their work done. Again, I found myself in a position where I had to adjust. I had to make new friends and find out what I was good at. The only subject I liked was math. I was good at math but I didn't excel in any other classes. I decided to fail because I didn't want to do all the other

## Devantae Butler

work. It was very difficult to me. I was a failing student until I was told I couldn't play football and basketball until my grades improved. Then I had to make a choice. I loved the game of football, but my academics didn't support that. During this time, I pouted hoping that someone would hear my cry and show me sympathy. I was ineligible three times during my middle school and high school years. I just wanted to play and not take my school work seriously.

Finally, things started to click with me going into the summer of my junior year. Our head coach at Gateway stressed grades very strongly. We all had mandatory study hall if our grades were under a certain GPA. I didn't want to be in study hall, so I got my grades together just so I wouldn't have to go. I received my 2.5 GPA, my highest ever and maintained that all the way until the second nine weeks of my senior year. Then a sudden change took place. I had a great senior season and was looking to go to college to further my football and academic career. I had already taken the SAT test twice and my score along with GPA made me NCAA eligible. All I had to do was finish through. I also played basketball after football season and felt that it was my time to shine.

Now I had been getting recruited during school hours every day for about two weeks straight. I missed tests, important notes, and lectures from teachers because of it. Three days before our first basketball game, our coaches checked grades. There was a new rule in place stating that if a student had two or more F's, then they were automatically ineligible during any period of the season. I had two F's because I was missing class. My teachers gave me zeros in the grade book until I made up my work. The coach told me I could not play but I was determined to play. Our game was on Saturday and that Friday after school I took my math and economics tests, which raised my grades from a 54% to 81%. I then went to the guidance counselor's office and made sure that they were changed in the system. They did, and I was good to go and play. I went into practice and showed my coach. He didn't

# Mindset

believe me and he told me,

"Go and get a principles signature for confirmation."
It was about 5:00 P.M in the evening on a Friday night. I said to myself, *There aren't any principals still in the building.* But without hesitation, I ran down to the office, and sure enough, there were two principals there. I smiled and said, "Yes!" out loud and explained what was going on. They signed the paper and I went back to my coach, however, he still didn't believe me. He stated that he would have to call him personally. I was confused at this point now. I know our coach didn't like football players who also played basketball but I did everything I was asked to do. I really wanted to play because we were facing LeBron James' old high school, St. Vincent-St. Mary's. So, the next day (game day) I asked the coach if he talked to the principal and he said yes but he wasn't going to play me. I began to get angry because I worked hard for the opportunity and I was hurt. During the bus ride, our entire basketball team had a Twitter account, and I stated something about the coach as a joke but it escalated. I got suspended from school for 30 days and kicked off the team. I was also banned from all home basketball games. I was so discouraged that I just gave up on everything. I had to keep my grades up for college football but merely finished the nine weeks with a 0.177 GPA.

    I barely graduated high school. I ended up walking with my graduating class but didn't get my diploma until I passed a test. I saw my future slipping away, and I didn't fight for it back. I let someone else get the best of me, not realizing how much my actions would cause me to look foolish in the end. The challenge for me was walking away. When things would happen to me, I always felt that I had to respond and defend myself because no one else would stand up for me but me. Now, I was a respectful young man and tried to do everything right when it came to athletics. I just wanted someone to take notice to my work ethic. The biggest problem in all of this was that I had no integrity at all regarding my academics. That was the root of the problem and I got in trouble because of my bad habits. If I had never slacked in

## Devantae Butler

school, I wouldn't have given the coach a reason not to play me because my grades would have been good. Maybe that was my lesson and I never realized it, that you can't just get by in life if you're not in agreement with the rules. I'm sure if given the chance no one would pay their cell phone bill. No one is given special discounts on a phone bill just because they have an iPhone. But because this was my mentality, I thought that just because I was an athlete I could slack in school. I soon understood the depth of the term student-athlete, however, I didn't apply it until it was too late.

    I was supposed to play college football, but I never got the opportunity to play a single down all because I wanted success, but my actions displayed failure. Never let a person or circumstance dictate your future even though you feel like you're being treated unfairly. I should have never thought that two wrongs would make it right. I failed myself and most importantly my family, and I was forced to attend CCAC in the fall. You cannot let people get the best of you. I feel as though it is very important to control your emotions. Don't give people the permission to take you out of your character. Every bit of distress is meant to fuel you to a greater level and point. Embrace the challenge by living to fight another day; every situation does not need an initial reaction. You don't have to jump up just because someone says they want to fight you. Give yourself time to think about what is going on first before you engage. Weigh out every opinion before deciding one. Keep in mind everything has a time period, which is important. It is also helpful to gain insight on how and why you're feeling this way.

    I suggest getting a mentor. You want to make sure you're venting to the right people who will ultimately point you in the right direction. Deciding to fail is also deciding to not acknowledge your mistakes that can help you grow. We have to be honest with what the truth is about us. You do not have to be talented or extremely gifted to be successful, you just need work ethic. You control your effort, working hard is what it sounds like. I was a hard worker when it came to sports, but I approached school with

## Mindset

an average mentality. Yes, I am more passionate about football than English class. Even so, I needed English class to play football and football didn't need me. The game would still be played without me. The source of not accepting failure as an option is pride. When you hear the term pride, you follow up with effort. Give effort in everything you are involved in. Remember everything has a season. What I mean is, you're only in first grade for a certain time, then you move on to second grade. In high school you have coaches, but in college, you gain new coaches. The season is the time gap from one thing to another. Failure is also temporary. You are a winner. You must tell yourself that daily. Once I stopped telling myself I was a failure, I stopped reacting to failure.

**Devantae Butler**

# Chapter Three: What's Your Why?

We all have that someone or something that drives us and pushes us further than anticipated. What makes you, you? The world wants to know what you bring to the table when you wake up in the morning. So, what is your why? For many people, this question may result in a specific family member or lost loved one. What is a why? A why is something you represent, something that is bigger than what you are standing for. There is always something greater that can push us to want more. We must seek that next level. Often, people give up because they haven't found something stronger than them to keep them going when challenged.

Your why will distance you from the group. You must be able to identify that your goals are more important than whatever or whoever is trying to invade your focus at some point. It is not a bad thing to enjoy yourself, but balance is important. Too much of anything isn't good, even for the most exceptional people in the world. You never want to get comfortable; don't slow down your own momentum. Keep it as high as possible. Your why is essential! Your why has an unlimited amount of value and can encourage you to reach a maximum place inside yourself that you never dreamed of.

I had a girlfriend, and she motivated me because she was too good for me. She was on the right track in her life. I believe her plan was to attend CCAC for a few years and transfer. So, I followed her and did the same. I felt as though, she was the one person in my life who cared about my future. She wasn't from where I was from, and our backgrounds growing up were completely different. She really gave me another view on life. She was honestly my only motivation. I just wanted to prove to her I was worthy. During this period of my life, I really didn't want to be at the school I was at, because none of my friends attended it. I started to belittle myself. I really wasn't focused at all. Then,

# Mindset

things took a turn for me when I got a refund check. Never in my life had I seen that much money all at once. I always worked but only part-time jobs. That refund check was like six of my paychecks all at once.

I went to the mall and used that check to buy shoes and games instead of books and school supplies. After my first year, I was put on academic probation. In addition, my girlfriend was very attractive. She attracted some new men at the time who were simply handling their business. I however, was still figuring things out. We ended up breaking up, but the worst part about it was that I had scheduled all the same classes as her for the next semester. I know, bad idea, but I thought it was sweet at the time. I would skip class just so I didn't have to see her and then go to class just to see her. I realized that she was no longer my why, but the trouble was that I never took the time to established a new why. I ended up flunking out and losing my financial aid. My inability to get loans for school forced me to take a semester off.

I have four younger brothers and one day I came home and asked my little brother where his homework was. He was twelve years old at the time. Now my parents always told me,

"Son, your brothers will do everything that they see you doing."

I knew my little brother looked up to me. While I asked him the question, he looked me dead in the eye and said,

"You're not even in school so don't tell me to do my homework."

I was furious and thought about hitting him, but then I realized it was my fault. After looking myself in the mirror, I had to take personal accountability for putting *myself* in a position to subconsciously give my little brother permission to say that to me. Before I went to classes and I knew that I didn't want to be there. My reason for going wasn't good enough and it was depressing. There wasn't any value in why I attended classes, my only motivation was my ex-girlfriend who had left me. When that took place, I lost sight of why I was even at CCAC, which was because I had put myself there. I never made it personal or told myself that

# Devantae Butler

I was going there to do better. Now, I told myself that I was going so that I could get enrolled back into the school and I was going to finish school for my little brothers. They were my reason why. I never knew how much my brothers were paying attention to me, but that just goes to show that someone is always watching. This was going to take me outside of my comfort zone. I never truly had to face this before, because I always tried to get by in any way that I could.

I found out what I had to do to get back enrolled and found out that I would have to pay out of pocket. I was hesitant when I found out this news. I didn't want to do that. I realized that I had messed up all my funding for school. A part of me said, *Don't go back that's too much for nothing,* but then another part said, *Get it done.*

I didn't know what I needed to make this happen, but I knew my little brothers were watching and I had to find a way. This was a complete shift for me because I had to face my fears for the first time. My fear was being a 4.0 student because I thought being smart or a nerd wasn't cool. My past was soon coming to haunt me, but for my family's sake, I didn't want it to ruin my future. My little brother sparked something inside of me with that statement. I changed the way I heard him say what he said to me. It prompted me to get back into school despite what I had to go through. The best thing about everything that was happening to me was, I found my new "Why" and with it I was determined to make my little brothers proud of me.

My brothers inspire me to go above expectations and reach a better version of myself. If I were to ask you, what's your why? What keeps you going during the times you want to give in? What strengthens you, even when you're weak? What will have you continuing to move forward, even when you want to stop? Your reason why promotes dignity in what you are doing. It is so important to indicate what the answer is for you. It will help you become persistent in anything that you are doing. Once this occurs, you will be able to perform at a high level, and you will have more urgency in your actions. Determine your reason why so

## Mindset

that you know why you cannot collapse when under pressure. Make sure it's something worth giving up everything for. Remember people come and go but a why is here to stay.

**Devantae Butler**

# Chapter Four: Turning Point

When I turned sixteen I got my license. I was so excited that day. Being influenced by my friend Darrell to get my license, finally receiving it felt good. The next thing I needed to do was get a car. Now my family didn't have a lot of money, so asking for a car was the last thing I was going to request from my parents. My parents did allow me to drive their car, but they had a van. I didn't see myself driving a mini-van, but then I thought about the fact at least I can drive something. Out of all my friends in high school, my friend Darrell had his license first, and he had his own car. We would drive our friends around all the time whenever we went out. I remember taking my parents car and picking up my teammates and just going to party.

Eventually, my dad bought me a car and gave it to me after graduation. This new gift made me feel extremely happy. I recall my dad specifically telling me,

"Son driving is a privilege."

But I didn't listen. I got speeding tickets and parking tickets. When my dad found out that I wasn't doing what I should have been doing, he took the keys to the car I thought was mine. All I started telling myself was that I needed my own car but what I should have been thinking about was the lesson my dad was trying to show me. I stopped focusing on the lesson to be learned, and I became more concerned about how to get my own. Therefore, I began working hard. I got two jobs and really pushed myself. I was livid when my younger sister purchased a car before me. I told myself that I had to get on my game immediately.

When I was twenty years old, I bought my first car. It was a maroon *2004 Chevy Malibu* from *Century III Kia*. The best feeling

## Mindset

in the world was coming out of a dealership for the first time with a vehicle I could call my own. The first thing I did was go to Wal-Mart and buy Drake's new album (Nothing Was the Same), until I got an aux cord. I couldn't wait to show it off. My brother Deion and I went all over town in my new car. This was a blessing that I never asked myself was I ready for.

Around that same time, I aspired to put together an event for my close friend who passed away when I was in high school, Darrell Turner. It was always placed in my heart to do something like that because I wanted to keep his name alive. Not only was he a close friend, but he was the one who influenced me to get my license in the first place. So, my mentor at the time happened to be best friends with a club owner who had his own venue in Oakland. I had plans to meet up with him to plan an event that I wanted to throw. I had the meeting and found out all the details that I needed to conduct this event and see my vision through. I was determined. I put down a financial deposit and began promoting the event. I had one more meeting with the owner to put down the rest of the money which was scheduled for a Friday night, but on that Thursday, my brother and I decided to go out. It was college night at *Whim* nightclub. We had smoked and drank beforehand. As we were leaving the club, we sat in the car about to conclude our night. That's when police officers knocked on my window. They were demanding me to get out of the car, stating that they smelled marijuana. I was arrested that night, and my vehicle was towed. They took all my money, my cell phone and a bag of weed. Throughout my time in jail, I asked myself, *How did I get here? Hanging with the wrong crowd*. Feeding off of negativity really got me into trouble. My time in jail made me think a lot because I couldn't do anything else. I didn't have my cell phone, I couldn't watch T.V., go outside, or anything! I was released at

# Devantae Butler

9:00 pm Friday night, the meeting for the club was at 9:30 pm. I managed to make it to Oakland and lock in my date for my party, but I lost my job because I had to work that morning and didn't show up. So, this event was the one opportunity that was placed on my heart to do. I worked really hard and made a real commitment to having the event that I called "Flashback." All my friends from high school, now in college, showed up and supported. The event was amazing. It showed me a lot about myself and what I could do! After the event, I came to my senses and recalled that I was unemployed. That's when reality started to set in. The money from my event was going away fast, and I needed money. One day my friends asked me if I would drive them up to Edinboro University to see a few females and they would pay me. I really didn't want to drive, let alone go, but I really needed the money, therefore, I agreed. It was five of us total and I let my friend, Dondi, drive. Edinboro was two hours away and I just wanted to relax.

    It was early February and winter time in Pittsburgh was crazy. We were about an hour into the ride before our lives would change forever. We were going 80 mph on the highway, and before we knew it, we skidded on some ice and the car spun out. We hit a guardrail and took out thirty feet of it. All I remember was waking up outside the car, and I couldn't move my body. I was severely injured. I broke my ribs, pierced my lungs (was on a breathing machine), and broke my ankle. As I laid in the emergency room, my brother Deion stood over me. I asked him,

    "How?"

    "I prayed." He answered.

    At that moment, I knew that God had spared my life. I began to reflect. I realized then, that my last conversation with my parents wasn't good because we had argued. When I was in the

## Mindset

hospital, my parents were the first ones there. I couldn't help but to break down at that moment and cry. I thought I'd never see them again. They displayed unconditional love and unity that day. This opened my eyes to a lot. I decided to change my life forever at that moment. When I came home after being discharged from the hospital, I had to depend on my family's help to function around the house. Even my little brother, who was four years old at the time, helped me out and really reminded me why I had to keep fighting.

Now at this time, I was twenty years old and living life at a fast pace. Never had I slowed down once to ever think about how I truly wanted my life to be. During this turning point in my life, not being able to do roughly anything, I spent a lot of time in bed reflecting on my life. I asked myself scary questions such as what would people have remembered me for if I would have died? What did I stand for, and how was I making an impact in other people's lives? I didn't like my answers to my own questions and I took it extremely hard. I was very apologetic to my family because I knew that I was an inch away from death. God's grace had kept me alive and I spent the majority of my alone time with him. After searching myself and evaluating my heart, I came to the conclusion that I had purpose. I never viewed my life as purposeful before, I suppose I just lived life and thought nothing major of it. After digging deeper into the reason why I was placed in this situation, I made a decision that would change my life forever! I made a declaration to myself to live my life every step from this point on with a purpose. My drive to live went up at this point. I respected it and took pride in my life now. The problem is, I thought I had already done this in the past, but this was at a higher level of respect and pride.

## Devantae Butler

    This time I wanted to redefine my life by striving to be the best me I could possibly be. I wanted my family to meet the Devantae who actually tries, gives his best effort, and who doesn't make excuses. I wanted them to know the real me. I placed this imaginary chip on my shoulder that said I can't do it. Therefore, I put my best effort forth because I pictured someone or something telling me I can't do it. This car accident was the biggest WAKE UP call I had ever received. I couldn't take my life for granted anymore because I understood that tomorrow isn't promised. I think we all lose sight of some things in life, which is natural. Just don't let the fact that you lost something make you unappreciative of everything else you do have.

    Tell your loved ones how much you love them every chance you get. Don't let days go by without speaking to them. Respect life for what it has given you, good or bad, while understanding that if you don't like what you are seeing you can change the atmosphere. Don't allow your current situation to take over your future. The cause for any turning point is for you to return to your foundations and get back to the roots of who you are. Everyone needs to be reminded of who they are and what their task is. There is no need to put added pressure on yourself. Just move forward and do not take anything for granted. Ask yourself, how many people do you know that get a second chance at life?

# Mindset

## Chapter Five: Be the Example

    After healing up, I started an organization known as *Reaching New Dreams & Recognizing Talents*. Now let me remind you, I aspired after high school to do an event for my friend/teammate who passed away in 2011. I called him my brother because we did everything together and I looked up to him. His death really hurt me and caused me to speak up more and become a better leader. After having my first initial event followed by my car accident, I decided to continue with what I was building. During this time, I also remembered what my little brother said to me about college and I wanted to go back for him. The question was how was I going to do it? In 2014, I had two events in the summer, a pool party and a glow party that were both sell-out events. I was receiving a lot of help from different friends who really were supportive of what I was doing. Then my brother stated to me that I should put a team together.

    My initial response was, he's right, I knew the value of having teammates because I've been a part of different sport teams my entire life. I wanted my team to be a reflection of my brother Darrell Turner, who had passed away. I believed he had great morals such as work ethic, love, and leadership. I was excited about moving forward with the vision I had. I started the group after my fourth event in August. We were a young group of college students looking to make an impact in our generation. We planned and conducted safe college events for our peers. None of this was easy at the same time. I was still conducting an organization which was completely new for me. I always appreciated my team for their dedication and support. I was still learning and developing during this time. I had to embrace my

## Devantae Butler

own process. I remember planning our first event as a team. We were planning a Black Friday party in November for the college students coming home for Thanksgiving break. The amount of preparation that went in was great; we had meetings consistently and everyone was excited about the event. The organization really helped me boost my confidence in speaking because I knew I had to be the voice for my own project. The event was going to be held at a hotel. I was on top of things, making sure that I did everything and was ready to go. I had booked the venue back in August. Now originally, the event fee was $1500, and that was all we had in our budget. I met with the event planner at the hotel, and she gave me a tour of the venue. It seemed as though we were both excited about the event. I had told my team how the first meeting had gone and we continued to add more ideas to our vision. Now a month prior, I met with the event planner again and I put down a deposit and signed the contract.

    She had informed me that once payment was paid in full, she would sign on behalf of the hotel. I agreed and we began promoting. This was going to be a big event, I encouraged my team to do their best and that their hard work would get rewarded. With that mentality and a team beyond me, I knew we would be successful. I remember our very first meeting. I typed a quote on our meeting agenda. It said, "Coming Together is the Beginning, Keeping Together is Progress, and Working Together is Success." My team believed in me and I wanted to be the best leader I could be. I knew that this would take time. A few weeks away from the event, the hotel's event planner informed me that there was a sale's tax that had to be added to the cost.

    "What was the amount?" I asked her.

    "Five hundred dollars." She answered.

# Mindset

I was discouraged because I knew we didn't have that money I only had $1500 to give. I went to the mall that day feeling depressed and frustrated. I sat at the mall for about an hour just thinking about every outcome and not once did I figure out how we would come up with the money. Next thing I knew, my brother D.J. came to the mall and he asked me what's going on? I told him and he quickly suggested to me to ask the team for support. This was so big for me in my life because I'm a Taurus and I am very stubborn and prideful. So the thought of me asking others for help never crossed my mind because it isn't something I do.

I knew my team was depending on me, so I felt that I had to deal with that on my own. This lesson showed me how important it is to ask for help. Do not think that because you are asking for help your value goes down. Everyone needs someone and I needed my team. I brought it to my brother's attention, Gregory Coleman; he helped me get the money. I was in relief the next meeting. We attended as a team and it felt so good counting the money out to her for the final payment.

Then, ten days away from the event I received a phone call from hotel management, and they informed me that my event would not be able to take place.

"Why?" I asked.

They answered that it was because of a security issue. Also, students who were under the age of 21 could not be around alcohol. They ultimately called it a "Flyer Party" and viewed it as a threat to the venue. I was hurt and upset because I had done everything right. In life, you just want to feel accepted. Well at that moment I felt rejected and I wanted to know why. I kept fighting and when speaking to the hotel event planner again, she told me that the alcohol was the biggest concern. As a result, I

## Devantae Butler

told her that we can eliminate the alcohol and when I shared that she immediately said the price would be doubled with more security. The venue price was already $2000, now the hotel requested $4000.

    I went back into depression because nothing was going as planned. I didn't know how to tell my team because they had all worked so hard. As I was lying on the couch, my brother Gregory continued to encourage me. He would wake me up every morning saying, "She signed the contract, it's going to happen." Now at the time, I thought he was crazy, but literally, he would say it every morning to me. It motivated me to get up and fight back so that's what I did. I called a lawyer and told him the situation. We set up a meeting with the hotel a week before the event. The first meeting went okay, but they still were sticking to the $4000 price; nothing had changed. We spoke again. My lawyer and I set up another meeting two days later to meet the hotel staff. When my lawyer started to talk, they immediately got up and left the table. That was the final confirmation. They weren't worried about the terms and conditions of the contract. We weren't having the party there.

    Just five days away from the event, they had cancelled my biggest project yet. I sat at the table with my head down beginning to weep, feeling like a letdown, but then my lawyer placed his hand on me and in a soft voice he said everything is going to be okay. My heart began to come into agreement that everything would be okay. At that time, I didn't know what to do. As I went home to pick up Gregory to tell him the news of the meeting, we took a drive to go get some food. Suddenly, I received an anonymous phone call from a lady, and she asked me was my name Devantae.

    "Yes ma'am." I answered.

## Mindset

She asked if I was looking for a venue to have an event I quickly answered,

"Yes!"

Right there in that moment, we received another venue and switched the date from Friday to Saturday.

On the day of the event, my brother sat me down to share a poem that he had written. It was entitled, *To Be Great*. The poem showed me that everything I had experienced was what comes up against great faith and belief. As long as you stand firm in what you believe, ultimately nothing can stop you. I realized that I was being tested in those moments to rise as a leader, and to think and be positive. It's not over until it's over.

We had the event and the turnout was amazing. The venue was bigger and better than the hotel we had originally booked. Following this, I found out what I had to do to get back into college. I was determined to finish for my little brothers and be a positive example no matter what. I found out that it wasn't cheap but I established a new "why" for what I was doing and it was greater than my feelings. I used my college parties to fund my education. It cost $2000 a semester to attend community college as a full-time student. I paid for four semesters and didn't have any books for any of my classes. I couldn't afford them because I had to get my own way to school. I had to put gas in my car all the time plus feed myself. My professors questioned me when I stated that I didn't have any money for books, I was not receiving any financial aid and I was my own financial support. They asked me how I planned on passing their courses. They didn't realize that my mindset was different now and I wasn't going to allow anything to get in my way from succeeding. For two years straight, I maintained a 3.0 GPA and could transfer to any school I desired. I reached my goal and had just enough credits to transfer.

## Devantae Butler

Once I realized that, I needed to shift my area of focus to something greater than myself. I was able to push myself further.

"Different circumstances present different outcomes," is something that a good friend would always tell me. My dad also pointed out the fact that my little brother and sister would do everything that they saw me do. I knew that finishing school was important because I had to set the bar for them. The bottom line was that if I didn't do well then, they would have an excuse not to do their best. Once I began to apply myself in school, I did better. I actually did homework and looked over my notes. "You can never fail a test that you are prepared for," a man once said.

As I reflected on the difference between my past and my present self, I acknowledged one word which was the difference, and that word was effort. My effort wasn't there in the beginning and because of it, my results were below average. If you want the top results you must work hard in every aspect to accomplish those goals. Do not think less of yourself or let other people get in the way of your goals. You must do whatever needs to be done, because that will keep you from a setback. "Attitude reflects leadership." All leaders must lead by example and a leader always separates him/herself. Leaders must lead by example. That is the best way to get your organization or team together, by leading the way.

# Mindset

## Chapter Six: You Don't Matter

One day I watched a movie called *Coach Carter*. It was about a Richmond School and their basketball team that was going downhill. The school got a new head coach who was determined to make an everlasting impact on the basketball players' future. The first day at practice Coach Carter gave the students contracts filled with expectations to be on the team. He then stated that basketball was a privilege. Two players walked out, and the ones who stayed had to commit first before playing on the team. The players had to wear ties on game day, and they had to attend every class, in which they had to sit in the front row. They also had to maintain a 2.3 GPA. The team was off to its best season in school history with Coach Carter (they were undefeated). That is, up until the players' progress reports came back and most players were failing and falling short of the contracts criteria. Because of this, Coach Carter locked the gym and forced his players to meet at the library to study together. One player stood up in defense of himself and said:

"I have a 3.2 GPA!"

Coach Carter responded and asked if he scored all the points for the team as well. The point Coach Carter was trying to make was that they win as a team and they lose as a team. Winning basketball games was not Coach Carter's primary focus, he wanted his players to get an education and go to college. Not one player was above the next. It was a team goal. Once they understood that they had to individually achieve their goals so that they could play again, they did. Almost everyone on the team went off to college instead of statistically going to prison or ending up dead. From this movie, I realized that people naturally

# Devantae Butler

wanted to be a part of something and no one wants to be alone. When you're part of a team, organization, club, or even family you must be willing to put others before yourself. A great team has no selfishness in its identity. Within our organization, we live by this quote that states, "Alone we can do so little, but together we can do so much."

Leadership is very important, and it can be the difference between success and failure. When you think about great leadership, you think of people who make an impact in the lives of others. When you are a leader, you must be willing to die to yourself, which means that you no longer matter. There is something bigger than you that takes priority. Jesus, the greatest leader I know, teaches us this through his examples to come and serve. Jesus would wipe the feet of his disciples, and in doing so, they drew closer toward his leadership. How you treat others is critical; you don't want to take orders from someone who treats you badly. Sometimes as a leader, you have to give up who you are in moments to allow others to recognize their value. Once your team members or staff see the importance of their own value, then that is when your team will become more effective. Then the entire group shines, the leader shines too. Let me share this short story of what I mean.

Our organization plays in almost every basketball summer league in Pittsburgh. The most recent league we played with was the JCC. There is some pretty good competition in that league. Our group had set a goal at the beginning of the year, and we said that we would win the JCC League. Now we battled in two tough playoff games and made it to the championship. We played the best team, and they had five division one athletes. It was a close game down to the wire. We were tied up with two minutes to go; then the team came down and made a three-point shot. I

# Mindset

answered back and I made a three-point shot to tie the game back up. They came down and shot the ball again, but they missed. We got the rebound, and the ball was in my hand. Now immediately I thought to attack, but after realizing the time on the clock and how hard my team had fought to get back into the game, I called a timeout. In the huddle, I knew that the other team was going to key in on me, so I designed a play for another one of my teammates. I told him that once he used the screen, we would make space on the floor for him to attack, but if they double teamed him, he would have to pass the ball for a better shot. We came out of that timeout with 40 seconds left on the clock holding for the last shot. The play worked out just how I envisioned it. We knocked down the shot and won the game. That moment was so special to me, because I was unselfish in such a key moment of the game. I didn't demand the ball like I wanted to, and we won. Instead, I died to myself and made a leadership decision that not only won us the game, but boosted the confidence of my teammates.

In the movie *Drumline,* one of the characters, Dr. Lee, had a phrase that he said. It was "One band; one sound," meaning, no one is more important than the band; no one is above anyone else. Everyone has a role to play, and that's what makes the band complete. These examples helped me with my mindset in understanding that I don't matter. What mattered was my little brothers seeing me graduate college and being successful in my career. If all a person sees is failure, then the next person is more likely to fail. As an older sibling you must understand that you are being watched closely by your younger siblings. Set the bar high! Therefore, when you feel like giving up, not studying, or finishing strong think about the people who you are really letting down. I learned how to become selfless. When I make decisions, even

## Devantae Butler

though my parents aren't around, I ask myself, would they be okay with this or what would they say? You know the answer, so start to think your decisions through.

I run a program through a middle school, and one day I asked my student,

"What are your weaknesses in school?"

He replied and said,

"When I get mad I walk away from teachers and out the classroom."

I then asked,

"When you apply for a job and get hired do you think when your boss gets on your nerves that you can just leave work?"

I continued to ask questions,

"What if you have a son who is two years old and depending on you, do you still leave work?"

He said,

"No because I have a responsibility."

"It is your responsibility to do your best at all times. You don't matter because your legacy is more important than your current situation."

I said to him,

"Remember someone is always depending on you to do the right thing."

**Mindset**

## Chapter Seven: The Power of Change

Change doesn't come easily, however, change is necessary when it comes to our dreams. There were a few areas in my life that I knew if I wanted the results, it would require more from me. My mentor once told me that, "Discipline is the bridge between good intentions and accomplishments." I needed to discipline myself to change. I realized that change starts from inside. In order to see better, I knew I had to be honest with myself, so I wrote down my strengths and weaknesses. This exercise helped me to be truthful with myself, because you must be able to take personal accountability when it comes to making a change for yourself. I had to be able to admit which things did not contribute to making me successful in certain areas.

I soon realized the biggest thing I had to change was my group of friends. Let me just say this; everyone is not your friend. I associated myself with guys who had no vision or sense of direction. They were students who didn't take school seriously. So, I became a product of my environment and I didn't take school seriously. I had to make some serious adjustments to change my life. Growth is a process. Things do not happen for you overnight, so please embrace it. I learned not to give up on myself when things got tough. It's easy to quit and it is harder to keep going. It's easy to play video games and harder to study. Why is that? We subconsciously tell ourselves at time that we will get to things later but we prolong important tasks, which is referred to as procrastination. I used to view change as bad, therefore, I always distanced myself from it. I developed the most consistent thought process and I was not willing to try new things, even in small areas such as new foods. I never admitted that I was the problem and

## Devantae Butler

that's the first thing you have to do in order to go higher. For me, to fix that issue I had to change my thought process. I had to change my priorities. Some of those changes meant doing homework before playing video games and studying before talking to friends on the phone. Life is about adjustments. When you can change the areas in your life that were leading you nowhere, that's the first sign of growth. Growth is your responsibility and no one else's.

I was never a big reader in school or in general. Every time I read something, I would fall asleep or doze off because I told myself that this is boring. As a result, I was never able to change that until I decided to change it. I stopped thinking about the negatives of reading and acknowledged the positive side. How we view things has a lot to do with our outcome. I viewed reading as boring, therefore, every time I would start reading I would shut down since that was my mentality. Reading materials possessed wisdom and information that I would always overlook. A wise man once stated that there is power in knowledge, however, being able to activate the knowledge you have is true power.

Once I took notice of the value of a book that I was reading, I made a step toward positive change in myself. Mahatma Gandhi once said, "Be the change that you wish to see in the world." That quote is powerful because change is a hot topic everywhere. People complain about things and want to change the situation but they just complain. True change occurs when you sacrifice the old you for the new you. You must be willing to help yourself grow, so that you can change your circumstances. There may be something that happened in life that you cannot change, but personally you can always change you. I had to remind myself that with growth comes change. What have you seen in your life that you felt wasn't right? For me, I took

# Mindset

notice of one specific issue from when I was a freshman in high school. I went to Gateway High School in Monroeville, a great school district in Western PA. There were kids from all over, with different backgrounds and ethnicities. Personally, it wasn't easy being a freshman, it was like you had to prove that you fit into a specific crowd. As a freshman, all you wanted was to find acceptance. Well for me, I was looking for acceptance in the popular crowd. I looked up to most of the football players at Gateway. They were some of the top athletes in the state. Nearly all of them attended Division 1 schools on scholarship. That was my dream to play college football and make it to the NFL. I truly felt honored to be around these guys. The only problem was, they picked on me instead of helping me. None of those guys encouraged me the way I felt a leader should. It went from me being excited to see them, to literally trying to stay out of their way.

    The worst part was that it had a strong influence on me. It was affecting the way I treated new students. I didn't realize until later that I was giving out the same hurt that I had received because my thoughts were *this is how it goes*. I believe that if those leaders had encouraged me to raise my grades and just took the time to redirect me to positivity, then my academics would have been better. When playing a sport, there may be hundreds of fans spectating but we still somehow find that one person of importance in the stands. That one person can make a difference because they are there for you. It only takes one spark for a car to start and you never know if you're called to be that in someone else's life.

    I realized that when an individual turns down help or doesn't see that they can make an impact in a certain moment, that individual has a selfish mentality. This is a common thing

## Devantae Butler

because we all get caught up in our own conditions and we don't acknowledge others in need. Other times, we may not feel that we are the right person to help someone else because of our own circumstances. It isn't easy to reject the feelings telling you that you can't be a benefit to someone else, but when you do that is true courage. Telling someone the right way to do something so that they can learn from your mistakes will ultimately grow the next generation. People are not thinking like this anymore, which I identified as the problem.

    When my teammate died, I was a senior but there were also freshmen who were affected by his passing as well. I knew that I had to comfort them as much as I needed it as well. His death brought us together at a higher level than ever before. It forced me to become a better leader and I helped underclassmen become more. The entire senior class stepped up and aided during this time of need. These examples really helped mold my step into the problems I felt needed changed. Do not be selfish with your wisdom because that's the secret to gaining more. Knowledge is everywhere you go. Begin to believe that you are the impact someone else needs first so you are always mentally ready. Change can happen in a moment, you must seize it. Great people do not wait on an opportunity, they create one. Seeking purpose by creating purpose in every area of my life enabled me to change my past ways. If you don't like where you are at, if you believe there is more for you, then change your current state by simply deciding to move forward.

# Mindset

## Chapter Eight: Make a Decision

In 1988 in Dallas Texas, a high school football team was projected to win it all. The team had incredibly talented athletes. The coach was hard on them because he used football as a tool to shape their character to become better men; that was his goal. One of the athletes named Jesse Armstrong was put on probation for stealing a tee shirt. He had a conversation with his coach and his head coach stated that, "You cannot replay your life so make good choices the first time."

Later, the football team was unable to play because of academic ineligibility. The team ended up winning the state championship despite all the adversity they had been through. Most of the seniors received Division 1 scholarships to continue to play football and further their education. These players had it everything all laid out for them, until three of them decided to start stealing from restaurants. Another player found out, and he wanted to steal with the crew as well. They asked Jesse Armstrong to join, but he declined. Later down the road, the players' actions caught up with them and five of them were arrested. The judge ruled that they all do around 12-15 years in prison. They never played the game of football again. Jesse Armstrong, however, played eleven football seasons in the NFL. This is a powerful story because the difference between these two circumstances was eleven seasons in the NFL versus twelve years in prison. For Jesse Armstrong, it came down to one decision. He had the opportunity to join his teammates, but he was not influenced due to the message his coach told him first. Life is about decisions; it is the choices we make that set us apart from others.

In every decision you make there is a consequence, good or bad. The question you must ask yourself is, can you live with the consequences of that decision? My dad bought me my first car in high school. My dad always told me, ever since I was a kid, he said,

"Son, when you're good you get rewarded, when you're bad you don't."

My father taught me right from wrong at a young age. When I was learning how to drive, he told me that driving was a privilege, not just with the law but with him as well. One day, I was planning to go out Saturday night to party with my teammates. I planned on driving and I asked my dad in advance. He said,

"Yes."

This was planned with two weeks' notice. On Friday, I asked him if I could use the car to see a friend. He said,

"Yes, but be back at 9 pm."

Therefore, I went to see my friend, but I knew my time was close to being up. They asked if I wanted to play the new *Madden* video game. I didn't have the game because it had just come out. I wanted to play so bad, so I stayed a while longer. I got caught up in the game. When I checked my phone, it was 11:00 pm. I rushed home, and my dad was waiting. I knew I was in trouble and because I was late he didn't let me use the car to go with my friends the next day. My dad was very strict on teaching me life lessons, so I didn't make the same mistake twice. I decided to stay at my friend's house on Friday, so now I had to deal with the consequences of not driving because I didn't stick to the agreement that we had made. What happens when you don't do

## Mindset

your homework? You don't get points or credit. It doesn't matter the reason. All the teacher wants to know is did you do it, or not. I realized that I wasn't making smart decisions when it counted. Mistakes will be made because no one is perfect, but the key is to learn from it.

    My dad was determined that I learned from the decisions I made. That's when I knew that there was power in making decisions. Every great leader must make tough decisions. People avoid them because they don't want the responsibility that comes with it. We cannot be afraid of those feelings/emotions, even if the choice you make is wrong. The truth is that it is even more valuable because it teaches you how to be better. Life is the biggest risk that we take boldly every day, not truly realizing that we make a million decisions daily. Even though these decisions are made through our subconscious, we decide a lot when you think about it, from waking up, to going to the bathroom, to checking your phone, or clicking on social media apps, etc. There are plenty of choices we decide on daily. The key, however, is to become an intentional decision maker. We want to develop better habits for ourselves that exemplify a better lifestyle pattern for our future. We want our good habits of making right decisions to form a behavior which becomes who we are. Building this up will create less stress for making bigger decisions. The small choices we make add up. Just think about all of the poor decisions we make, like deciding to lie, or not doing our homework, or showing up late to school. These things only lead to terrible decision making. You become what you repeatedly do, therefore, you always want to hold yourself accountable to the choices you make, good or bad.

**Devantae Butler**

## Chapter Nine: There Is a Difference

What is the difference between a job and a career? A job is something that pretty much anyone can get with little to zero knowledge of the field they are applying for. Almost everyone who seeks a job is seeking money first, with no interest in helping the company first. How many of you would volunteer your time at McDonald's? The only time employees get excited about a job is on paydays. Now let's focus on a career. A career is something you have experience in. People who have careers are passionate enough about their work to seek more than just monetary value. People who have careers practice their craft consistently. There's a difference between people who know what they want vs. people who have no idea what they want. You must decide who you want to be first and how you are going to do it, then great things will happen for you.

What would you consider yourself to be good or great at? Average people are okay with the term "good job." They are satisfied with knowing that more could have been done. However, those who seek to hear "great job" are satisfied in knowing that someone recognized their full effort. After seeing the difference between good and great, I wanted to observe some of the greats to support this theory. Let's look at Carmelo Anthony vs. LeBron James. Carmelo is a good NBA basketball player. He can score any way possible. Unfortunately, he has a very low win percentage and no championship rings. Many would say that Carmelo Anthony is a good NBA basketball player. LeBron James is a great player. He has been in the NBA championship seven consecutive times. The difference is not in a person's physical nature but what lies in their heart. Consistency should be your best friend when

## Mindset

you're chasing after personal growth. You must be unselfish. An unselfish person is powerful. To not only live or do for yourself but for others is the solution to a better place. When you're doing something for yourself, it is one thing, but doing something for others is another. I believe that mothers are the greatest specimens on earth. They know that you must find what you are willing to sacrifice, in order to achieve something.

    My mom is a good person. She had me at a young age. She was an only child that didn't know too much about what family meant. She didn't have her father in her life, and her mom wasn't as present as she would have liked. When my mom became pregnant with me, she made a conscious decision to make sure that I had more than what she had. I appreciate my mother so much because she sacrificed her dreams and replaced them with me. I became her new passion, her new schedule. She naturally became a better person by becoming a mother, simply because she was the only one who had the role of being my mother. She took pride in being a mother. She was determined to become the best version of herself for our family.

    The purpose is in making the sacrifice for others, not for yourself. Jesus died for us, not for himself. Love is the biggest weapon we all possess. By choosing to love someone with your fullest capacity, you can change someone's life forever. I mean just think, don't you want to be loved by the person you crave for loving you the most? Whether it's a parent or a friend, we all desire to be loved. You cannot love someone or something and be in an advantaged state of mind. When you love something, it pushes you further towards that better you. Anything that challenges you subconsciously persuades you to see more. The challenge is necessary; it will ultimately tell you where you are in your life. I have finally reached a point of knowing that the

## Devantae Butler

difference will always be self. How far are you willing to go to see change in your life? Do you believe that you have been holding yourself back all along? These are the questions I began to ask myself before I concluded that I wanted more from myself.

Mindset

# Chapter Ten: You Owe You

One of my favorite quotes is by Marianne Williamson. She talks about our deepest fear and the quote reads, "Our deepest fear is not that we are inadequate. Our deepest fear is that we are powerful beyond measure. It is our light, not our darkness that most frightens us."

For a long time, I blamed everyone else for the things that happened in my life, not realizing that I was running away from myself. I was a bad student and a bad friend for no other reason than I just wanted to fit in. I thought being cool would decrease my chances of being bullied and increase my chances of being popular. I never had a lot, and my parents did their best in keeping a shelter over my head and food on the table. I never had the best school clothes but didn't have the worst either. Still, I desired more. I tried my best to keep up with other kids but I lost sight of myself. Materialistic things were all I cared about growing up. My peers had a huge influence on that subject. I found out that what I lacked the most was confidence. I could never find the strength to stand up to my friends and say *who cares what someone has or doesn't have*. None of us were old enough to work anyway.

Confidence is important when you know your goals. Nothing will persuade you away from them. Being worried about clothes and shoes shifted my focus from where it truly needed to be, which was on my education and myself. I always viewed growth as reaching the next grade level, but that was not growth at all. When it was time to do homework, I waited until the last minute. I convinced myself that I didn't know how to study, so I didn't. When the test came, I always sat next to someone who

# Devantae Butler

was smart or got help from a friend. Next thing I knew I was addicted to never trying in school. This mentality led to me barely graduating high school. I couldn't go to the college of my choice, so I attended community college. I started to grow envious of my peers/friends because they attended colleges and universities that I couldn't get into. I started to get depressed. Not to mention, my ex-girlfriend had a big influence on me, and when we broke up, I felt empty, as if no one was there. I started getting involved with the wrong crowd of friends and before you know it I got suspended from the college. I landed myself on academic probation and lost my financial aid. A month later my little brother motivated me to look myself in the mirror. I discovered the truth about myself, even though I was afraid to hear the truth. I never gave 100% and never listened to the teachers/staff that cared about me. I was ignorant to love and respect towards myself. I created a series of bad habits for myself that made it seem like death or jail were my only options.

    When change came, I knew that I owed it to myself for all of the times I only half did things. I was determined to put pride into everything I did in my life from that point forward. I knew that I would have to be consistent in my actions. I would have to mean what I said and eliminate every excuse in my body. The only way to delete bad habits is to develop good habits. No more settling for average or just good. My mindset was set on greatness. I dared to see what it looked like and what my light looked like. You see when you have been in the dark for so long, you forget what light looks like. It was time to challenge myself and set goals. I became obsessed with taking steps towards my personal growth. You cannot be afraid to decide to want more. Change starts first with yourself; you cannot seek change out of your situation until you adjust your values. The biggest enemy we

## **Mindset**

face is self. I had to decide not to hold myself back any longer. The one thing we have full control over, if nothing else, is our effort. I was determined that my focus would be greater than ever before. Therefore, I worked on myself by reading more and writing. I eliminated my comfort zone and moved forward by being fearless. Once I discovered my gift through my passion and aspirations, I never looked back. I realized that I could inspire others through my actions and my words. Sports taught me a great deal on how important a voice was. I took advantage of every opportunity I could get to have my voice heard. I attended community events, meetings, panel discussions, or anything where I could be heard. My confidence in speaking came from me holding meetings twice a month with my team. I spoke to them as if I was speaking in front of a thousand people.

You must treat the small moments like the big moments. I wasn't afraid of my process to learn how to become better. Studying other speakers helped me as well. It made me appreciate my story and obstacles. Over the last three years, I have spoken over a hundred times. You must be relentless when you want to accomplish anything in life. I sought more out of myself and that is what I got in return! I used every mistake I had made, and I took it personally. I used my mistakes as a bridge for me to be successful in my goals. I was no longer concerned with the opinions of others. I pursued what was in my heart for the first time. Once I could see that people appreciated my work, it only inspired me to go that much harder. For a lot of us, we lack loving ourselves. We have been rejected for so long, that when it comes to things that we love we have to shrink. I tried to find acceptance in other people for so long, trying to give out love, but truth be told, I didn't love myself. Now, how do you learn to love yourself again? Change your mindset. Stop focusing on how to

## Devantae Butler

please everyone else and seek your own opinion. Do not consider what others think of you. Believe in what God says about you. You are special. It wasn't until I fully believed in those statements that I was able to see that I *was* special. To stop doubting yourself is a difficult thing to do, because sometimes we picture different outcomes that don't align with our vision. For example, I loved to sing; I always viewed myself as Usher, the R&B singer. One day in choir class, there was an opportunity to do a solo. Anyone could audition for it and the best male singer would get it. I wanted to do it so badly, but then the thoughts crossed my mind on what my friends would think. I didn't audition out of fear of others' opinions. I believe when you love yourself you don't hesitate when an opportunity is in front of you. We cannot allow others to steal our confidence. There is power in stepping outside of your comfort zone and following your heart.

Think about it like this, you have been given a gift that was specifically designed for you and only you. Some people's gifts may be speaking, dancing, writing, sports, drawing, etc. Once you identify your gift, you must protect it and realize that everyone doesn't have what you have. We must take pride in the fact that we can do amazing things. Sometimes we take what we can do for granted. Your gift and your happiness matter and they are so important for what you will leave on this earth. Understand that if you are struggling with overcoming something, that means there is another person just like you. By overcoming your comfort zone, you will automatically liberate others to leave theirs too.

Look in the mirror. You have been holding yourself back for so long. You have placed blame on other people and circumstances for so long that you stopped questioning yourself. Now is the time to face yourself and demand greater. Now is the time to stand up and fight for what you believe. You owe yourself

## Mindset

the love you deserve now. By doing this very thing, people will automatically value you more. Your value is low right now because you haven't established your own worth. For instance, when my grandma would call me handsome, I would be filled with so much joy but when I went to school and a girl would call me ugly it belittled me. It doesn't matter who compliments you and who rejects you. If you don't form an opinion of who you are you'll never reach your full potential. Increase your self-confidence; encourage yourself first. That way when you receive compliments your perception comes from the gratitude that someone truly took notice of who you really are. Loving yourself isn't easy; it's tougher than it sounds, but you can do it. You deserve what comes with it, and that is a prosperous life.

**Devantae Butler**

# Chapter Eleven: This is Your Journey

Influence is the number one thing that causes someone to believe in themselves or not. As human beings, understand we are all influencing others on a day-to-day basis. Now what we choose to do with that influence is our choice. Many people believe that friendship is based on loyalty and commitment. This can be somewhat true, but first, you must identify what you are loyal to and what you are committed to. Also, every great friendship or relationship, in general, requires sacrifice. It's not about meeting the right partner, it's about being the right partner. My mentor always said, "Love gives, and lust takes."

We must rearrange what we think. It's not always about what you can get out of something but what you can give. Be more willing to give and slower to take, because love is a weapon. Have you ever seen the movie *The Wizard of Oz?* This was one movie that I was raised on growing up as a kid. This movie has a lot of life lessons in it when you view it in a different perspective. Once I started seeking wisdom, I began to view everything that was in front of me in a serious way. *The Wizard of Oz* is a story about Dorothy. Now I want you to view yourself as Dorothy. Dorothy got into a disagreement with her Aunt Em, so she left out of the house. Then, a tornado came. I believed that this was ironic because Dorothy put herself in her own storm, just like we do to ourselves sometimes without even immediately realizing it. The next thing that happens is Dorothy wakes up to a world that she is unfamiliar with, but she is greeted with love.

All of the people that she met were happy to meet her, even though they did not know her. The first thing they gave

## Mindset

Dorothy were ruby slippers, but Dorothy didn't understand the significance of the slippers, just like we don't understand the significance of mindset and the value of thinking before we act. They asked Dorothy what she wanted, and she said to get back home to her aunt in Kansas. They told Dorothy that if she wanted to reach that place, "Then you must follow the yellow brick road." They told her that at the end of the road a great wizard could give her whatever she needed.

That yellow brick road was a road of discipline, commitment, and perseverance. In the Bible, in the book of Matthew, there's a scripture that talks about two roads. The first road is wide but it leads to destruction, and narrow is the other road, but only a few find it. This may sound funny just thinking about how easy it is to get distracted and how hard it truly is to stay focused, but often times in life it is more difficult to do what is right. In *The Wizard of Oz*, the people started to sing to Dorothy, "Follow the yellow brick road, follow the yellow brick road," in a constant tone that reminded her where to go. We need that constant reminder in our lives, positive people to pour into us and direct us towards that right path. Now the biggest thing next to realize is that Dorothy met the Wicked Witch and the she wasn't too happy about Dorothy wearing the ruby slippers. The Wicked Witch understood the value in the slippers. Sometimes when people see the value and potential in you, they try to block you from seeing it. In our own lives, the Wicked Witch represents negativity, adversity, obstacles, and anything else holding us back from reaching our goals. Before we take the initiative to start the yellow brick road journey, it is good to know what it takes for us to truly reach our destination. Once we decide to step outside of our comfort zones and embrace our road, we will discover purpose.

## Devantae Butler

    As Dorothy was walking, seemingly by herself, she met the Scarecrow. The Scarecrow was made of straw and wanted a brain. Using a man made of straw was important, because in the nursery rhyme of *The Three Little Pigs*, the Big Bad Wolf would "Huff and puff" and try to blow down the homes of the pigs. That nursery rhyme showed us the difference in foundations. Your foundation is what you stand for. We all know that a person that doesn't stand for something will fall for anything. If your foundation is built of straw, you will be easily moved when people try to distract you. However, if your foundation is strong like brick you cannot be persuaded to follow the crowd in life. Bringing it back to *The Wizard of Oz*, the Scarecrow also wanted to have a strong mentality. It's not an easy thing to stay loyal to what is important to you, especially when others don't see the importance of your mission. The Scarecrow believed in his mission, and asked Dorothy if he could join her on the yellow brick road. She said yes.

    Next, they encountered the Tin Man, but when they saw him, he was stuck in place. The Tin Man is a special character similar to you and I. He had a dream/vision. He was building towards it with his ax and one day as he was building the rain came and he was rusted in place. The rain, in this situation is symbolic for adversity. Anytime we want something, there will always be obstacles that comes up against that. The Tin Man was now stuck, and had lost his heart for what he was building. Dorothy and the Scarecrow noticed some oil nearby, so Dorothy asked, "What would you like me to oil first Mr. Tin Man?" He mumbled for her to oil his mouth. When they oiled his mouth so that he could speak, he then said that he had no heart. This is symbolic because, we too, must learn first how to speak up, but more importantly we must speak from the heart. We cannot be worried about what others think about us, we must open up and

# **Mindset**

be honest. When she asked him how he got like that, he said "Suddenly it began to rain, and right in the middle of a chop, I was rusted solid." It's so important to know that obstacles lie in everyone's life. The best way to defeat these obstacles is to face them. Life will test what you want, so you must be willing to fight for what you want. Do not let your trials in life defeat you, continue to believe with all your heart that you will get through! The Tin Man also continued on the journey down the yellow brick road with the Scarecrow and Dorothy. Then, they ran into the Cowardly Lion, who at first was attacking them by trying to scare them away. When struck in the nose, he immediately stopped. He started crying and acknowledged the fact that he didn't have any courage. A lot of us don't have courage to really do what we want. We let other people paint this picture of who we are instead of painting our own picture. Some of us don't have courage to study, courage to tell our friends the truth, courage to set goals, etc. We must face our fears in life, and sooner or later address the truth on what is holding us back. The four continued the journey together helping each other get through and they reached the end of the yellow brick road together. There, they met the wizard, only to find out that they had everything they needed inside of them all along. When you look at each character, you see how each was broken in different areas but wanting that same thing. We must discover people in our lives who are on the same mission as us, but the only way we will meet these people is by discovering what we want at the end of our yellow brick road journey. Your journey is your journey and no one else's. The best advice you can receive is focus on your ladder.

    When we focus on what others are doing we become envious in what they have. This is not good for your thought process. Only negative things can come from this. Be happy with

## Devantae Butler

where you are. Sometimes the areas where you are not comfortable are the very areas that will make you stronger. Your situation is meant to be. Your life isn't tough. Remember, it can always be worse. Success isn't scripted and there isn't a proper procedure for it. The ultimate goal is to take steps forward consistently. There will be many things that try to distract you, but allow nothing to stop you and stay faithful on your path. As much as the Wicked Witch tried to stop Dorothy, at the same time, she became stronger. Adversity fuels you to become more in that moment.

# Mindset

## Chapter Twelve: Separate Yourself

    Everyone is not the same, so why do people fall into the same category? As I was doing a study on Bishop T.D. Jakes, I discovered something about his ministry just by paying close attention to what makes him special. It is important to remain a student of life; never stop learning. That is the first key point that I discovered about Bishop Jakes. He wasn't just a teacher but a student as well. Often times, when in big groups we are asked the question "how many of us have dreams ?" Normally, a majority of the group, if not all, raise their hands. By raising your hand, you are identifying that you have a vision in your mind to reach something.

    My question is, if everyone raised their hands when they were asked about their dreams, but no one reaches them, then why did they raise their hand? The question the world wants to know is, what separates you from the rest? It is easy to have a vision or idea, however, it is harder to create a plan and follow through with it. People are intimidated of nothing other than themselves. My whole life, truth was based on the idea that I was my own darkest enemy. When you are trying to transform your life for greater, you must face your fears first. This is not easy to do since many of us have hidden ourselves under a shell because we let life get to us. Life has told us *no*, life has told us *we can't*, and life has told us *we aren't good enough*. It is all an illusion to cover up how amazing you truly are. The second step is, you need to separate who you are now from the past you. You need to create a plan and have a vision to be better and to get better. You

## Devantae Butler

need to focus on what you want to see and how you will fulfill these goals.

The third step is having integrity for yourself and your environment. We must be honest with where we are in life and respect it. I cannot say I want to be a great math student when I just cheat on tests and lack study habits. This is a very true example because sometimes we forget how important the learning process is, in order to get through things faster. Developing patience is important as well.

Number four is to commit yourself. What does it look like to be fully committed to your craft? When you look at any great CEO, athlete, or parent, they are committed to their vision. A committed person is unstoppable. Nothing can stop their pursuit. I think that's important to know, so that we don't look at others for confirmation in what we are invested in.

The fifth step is to believe. We must believe in ourselves to the fullest capacity. Allow faith to work for you when you cannot see a physical manifestation. Even when people doubt you, believe that it will happen for you.

Number six is big. It's to think and to be positive. Now I know it's easy to be negative, especially when that's the mentality of your environment, but you must separate yourself. You need positive people around you to support your positive train of thought. Whatever you tell yourself that you want to happen, will happen. We become what we dwell on. Your thoughts, just like your tongue, are powerful. We must learn how to take advantage of our positive minds. It is the deadliest weapon on earth. A positive mind can change the world.

Number seven is to be a leader. By just standing on your foundation of what's right vs. what's bad, you will have

## Mindset

unconditional influence over your peers. You can change an entire nation; the question is, will you? The separation comes when you understand that you are *in* the world, but not *of* it, meaning that you don't get caught up on what is trending or the negativity. Yes, you are aware of these things but because your calling is so high, you separate yourself from irrelevant things. When you decide to separate yourself, you are saying you're ready to be alone. You're ready to sacrifice what others aren't. You want to make the tough decisions, and you are extremely focused. You understand that your actions aren't for you any longer, and without knowing who you are doing it for, you push yourself as if you have known these anonymous people your entire life. Many will not take the journey that you are willing to take. That's because their pain isn't equal to yours.

Reflect on these seven steps to transform into something greater and ask yourself what they look like to you. America is a free country, however, it's waiting to see what you bring to the table. The world needs you to get over your hump so that greatness can be presented. Think about every great individual that you know. Let's just take a look at why you are inspired by them vs. someone else. Immediately, we see that there is something about them that sticks out to us. For instance, let's use Michael Jordan for example. To me, what sticks out about him is that he didn't make the basketball team in high school, but he didn't allow that to stop his dream. He then went on to become the greatest NBA player ever with a total of six championships. He had what I call willpower, which is the ability to continue to press forward even when something tries to come against how you feel. This goes to show everyone that if you want it, you can have it, but you must work towards it.

## Devantae Butler

My sister is one year younger than me. Her name is Dominique Harper. She has a twin brother named Dominick Harper. They both are special when it comes to making great decisions that separate them from others. My sister was a great student her entire life, I mean literally a 4.0 GPA student. She made it hard to bring report cards home to mom. I was curious on how she was doing this, so for about a week, I watched her. I knew what I did after school. I would come home, throw my clothes off, and play my video game all day. She came home, went right into her room, and took her books out. She immediately started working with no time to waste. Literally her bed was her desk. It was full of open books and homework papers. She trained herself to never be finished. She was always doing homework or studying. Even if she didn't have a test coming up, she was preparing herself for the future. I did not have this mentality and our report cards reflected it. I couldn't run from the fact that I wasn't really trying and my sister worked extremely hard to get her results. Hard work is hard work. It may look easy, but the reality is, it's not easy. It's a hard thing to maintain.

Dominick Harper, our brother, was very smart as well. He didn't fully apply himself in every area of his life, however, when it came to what he was passionate about, he was relentless. He had so many aspirations to do great things and he would always tell people he was leaving Pittsburgh to follow his dreams. They just thought he was talking, but he left and moved to California to put himself in a better position to achieve his goals. This is what the great people do, they take initiative and then they execute. The problem is, many of us have a vision for what we want, but we don't want to do what it takes to accomplish that vision. Stop over thinking your decisions. Everyone isn't meant to do what you are meant to do. Just remember when you display courage to go after

# Mindset

what you believe, you give others hope to do the same. Everyone has an opinion of you, so don't get caught up in other people's negative feedback. It's all designed to get you to question your choices. Therefore, we have to stand firm on what we believe at all times. Do not forget your foundation and remember to use the lack of vision others have for you to inspire you to go higher.

Separation is so important to being successful. sometimes you must leave others behind. If people aren't adding to your situation, then they are subtracting from it. This does not mean that they are bad people, but not everyone is qualified to be the CEO of Apple. You are your biggest investment and your own product. What's the difference between an iPhone and an Android? They are both phones; you can text and talk on them both. So what is the difference? Well the difference is the brand, that's what separates the two companies and ultimately the products. Now I want you to look at your life and ask yourself what you want. What will separate you from the next person? Develop a routine for greatness and make it become consistent to your life. Once you have these things, you will move completely different in your actions and your mentality. Think things through and don't settle for less. You are destined to shine, so be that light.

### Devantae Butler

## Chapter Thirteen: By Any Means Necessary

There is power in shifting your perspective. A motivational speaker once said that it's better to be prepared and not have an opportunity, than to have an opportunity and not be prepared. My question is, are your prepared for your moment? What will you do when it is in front of your face? What is the mentality you should have to accomplish something? I have discovered that great individuals have that "by any means necessary" mentality. They have the mindset that they will accomplish something without allowing excuses to interrupt their mission. I'm sure we have all been around someone who gets the task done no matter what it may be. That's the type of person that every strong company desires. The one attribute you need in order to possess that type of mentality is confidence.

People will say you can't do something just because their confidence is low. The most dominant person is someone who knows who they are and knows what they want. People who question you question themselves. Never let someone who lacks confidence in themselves steal yours. Individuals with confidence liberate others to find theirs through their example. Who is someone in your life right now who exemplifies a "by any means necessary" mentality? For me, it's my mother. She is extremely driven by her children and family. I've seen my mom in tough situations find ways to get it done. I had to observe her more. When I did, I found that the biggest thing my mom did in every moment of her life was that she always believed in something. She believed something different could happen.

She believed in Jesus. I see God elevate my mother through her faith. I have seen the tears, the storms, and the

## Mindset

results. Sometimes we are put through storms only to test our mental makeup and our hearts in those moments. You must stand on your faith, even when others lose theirs. My mom taught me to not depend on anything other than God because God keeps His promises. His word gives me great joy and confidence. He is the ultimate way-maker, therefore, the mentality that nothing will stop me or hold me back was established by using a foundation of faith. Faith will take you to greater places, places that your strength and knowledge cannot. Many people think that it is easy to have faith or just believe in something in general. However, what if your faith is tested? Being tested shows that there are levels to your faith. Your job is to identify what level your faith is on, because it matters. Yes, you should have faith in yourself, but how much faith do you have in the people who are around you? The people around you should support the level of where you are. The reason is because most of the time it is the people who are around us the most who challenge our faith, which means they really don't think you can do something fully.

    This is natural for people of vision. Great mothers have a vision for their children. They also understand that consequences come with having a vision. My mom was determined to move our family out of the hood and into a better neighborhood. She wanted better for our family, more than what she had. She understood that she had to give up, to go up. With great power comes great responsibility. She worked day and night to provide. My mom saved, what she wanted to spend, to make it happen. Faith without work is dead. You can't ask for a miracle and be afraid to move. When you are seeking to do the extraordinary, you must do the uncomfortable. It is easy for you to identify the gifts within others, but harder to see yourself. You must face what makes you uncomfortable for a moment in order to achieve

## Devantae Butler

something that will last. Be brave and stand in faith; do not reject your inner voice that is trying to encourage you to speak up or ask questions.

"By any means necessary" means you get results no matter what the obstacle may be. It means you are committed to finding a way out of excuses and into triumph. We need to have a change in our mentality to get to that next level. First we must fix our perspectives on how we view things. Only when we shift the way we think, will we be able to truly envision more. It's time to have your own sense of identity. Let's look at ourselves more, and ask the question that empowers us to accomplish what is in our hearts. Everyone has the ability to do so, all we have to do is tap into what is inside of us and be it! Stay focused on your goals and keep telling yourself *you are almost there*. I said this quote once, "When you focus on what you can see, you can't see further." This quote supports the fact that you are greater than your current environment. We all have greatness inside of us, it's about pushing it out. Once this is done, you are destined to be great. Many people will try and hold you back, just make sure you are not one of those people yourself. Execution is what will separate the vision you have for yourself, versus the opinion that others have for you. When you make up your mind to achieve something, you will have obstacles come up against you. Continue to be bold and courageous in everything you do, that's the ultimate key. You must respect the opinions of others because everyone will have an opinion. However, you're not forced to believe them.

Tom Brady is one of the best quarterbacks in the NFL, and his organization, the New England Patriots, has the most NFL Super Bowl appearances. The Patriots have experienced a lot of success as an organization, even so, there are a lot of teams and

## Mindset

people who do not like them. Some people called them cheaters, some called them winners. Regardless of all the negative comments they received, it never stopped their mission. When others can't do it, they will tell you that you can't do it either. Tom Brady understood his surroundings very well and he also knew that he had the final say so on his career and life. Tom Brady's mentality is so special because he continues to attack his own legacy. He is not worried about anyone but himself. He is focused on becoming better for his teammates. When pursuing excellence, there is no time to look back. Your past accomplishments are not relevant for the present time. People want to know if you are still striving for your goals today. You may have just told them yesterday, but they will still ask about it today. Tom Brady has the mindset that says, *I'm not finished yet*. So ultimately, no matter how long you have been in a career, job, or school, continue to tell yourself that you're not done yet. If you have ever wondered what it takes to be a champion, well, it starts with your thinking process. How you think in situations will improve your response. Be fearless in your willingness to execute and stay blind to the opinion of others. You only live once.

**Devantae Butler**

## Chapter Fourteen: Choose Wisely

So many times, I have heard people say, it's not what you know but who you know. Just like it's not what you say, it's what you do. In life, the most valuable thing is relationships. Who is in your corner backing you up as an individual? Your surroundings may be more important than yourself at times. Studies say, if you show me the five people you hang around the most, I can show you how successful you will be. I never understood the importance of the principles behind relationships. I was so used to getting people to try and accept me, that I lost sight of who I was.

The first significant key to finding healthy relationships with people is to find someone who accepts you for you. If someone is not able to appreciate who you are as a person then ultimately, they will not truly value you. I had this problem in high school. I was just looking for people's opinion for confirmation of things that I liked. When I didn't get the feedback that I was hoping for, I gave up. You cannot allow people to dictate who you are. My mentor once said to me, "Never allow someone who doesn't know who they are, tell you who you are."

The next key thing you need when looking for a great relationship is positivity. This is so important because you are what you think. So many people miss out on amazing opportunities and eliminate great moments out of their lives because they told themselves *no*, or *I can't*. This is not a great mindset to position yourself in. For example, in the movie *Remember the Titans,* the message of the film was all about rising above racism and how challenging it was to break the chain of discomfort between whites and blacks. In the movie, there were two defensive stars on the team. One was named Julius and the

# Mindset

other Gary. Julius was black; Gary was white and he was also the defensive captain. In the beginning of the movie, they were paired up to sit together on the team bus before camp. The entire team hated the new rules created by the coach, but the coach knew that to win, the team would eventually have to see eye to eye, and no longer see race or color. There had to be one vision and one goal. The two players didn't see eye to eye and the defense was suffering. They just continued to view their relationship as something negative instead of a positive. Both were stubborn and not willing to try to understand one another. By responding in this way, nothing improved between them.

Suddenly, one day at practice a good defensive play was made. Days before this, both players had a conversation that was controversial, but it sparked something. Gary, the captain, put down his fence and opened his heart to Julius. After deciding to be more positive for the team, the relationship grew into a brotherhood. Color no longer meant anything to the two players and because they made the decision to be positive, they liberated an entire community to do the same, including their families. The point is that when you have positive energy around you, you begin to see a shift in your momentum. Being positive will free your heart, because it protects you from your past and helps boost your future. Positive thinking is the difference between the possible and the impossible.

The next key feature you need when building relationships, is someone who challenges you. Most of us like being the "top friend." I know I did. I liked the feeling of having leverage over the relationship, but there are pros and cons to this. The good thing is that as the top friend you make the majority of the decisions, so the direction of the relationship is in your hands. The bad thing, however, is that there is no one to hold you accountable. What happens when you're not held accountable? Well from experience, I know it's easy to get lazy. You procrastinate more because no one is questioning you. These things are not healthy for your personal growth or development as a person. You should always challenge yourself by wanting someone to know your goals and ask you questions that you haven't considered, but we all run away from that at times because of doubt that penetrates our minds.

    As a kid, I never had to worry about the rent or how I would pay the bills. I had my mom for that. Now I am sure that she had those concerns at times, but what would it look like to have an 11-year-old kid ask you about the rent? I can see it now, me asking my mom,

    "Hey Mom, did you pay the rent this month?"

    Her immediate response might be to hit me then make me go to my room and turn off all the lights. Truth is, my mom is my leader, and it's just not my place to ask her that question. Now because my dad is more equal to my mom, they could challenge each other. If rent is split down the middle, that means that I need your half, just as much as you need mine. Automatically there is accountability between both of them, because there is an equal relationship, as opposed to the scenario with one person being the "top friend." This makes it easier for my dad to question my mom instead of me. Some of us don't like the pressure of being held accountable and someone knowing what you have to do, but the advantage is that someone can remind you to stay focused on your "A" game.

    The next trait we need in relationships is so important, it's love. Love is the most dangerous weapon we all possess. It is the very thing that gives the poor wealth and the weak strength. People who do things for you in acts of love brighten up your day.

## Mindset

Love is an unbelievable joy we feel on the inside that makes us want to give it to someone else. One day I was so angry, and I was upset because I was getting bullied by some so-called friends. I felt empty and unworthy. As I sat by myself not wanting to talk, someone came up to me and asked me if I was okay, I said,

"Yeah."

But they could tell I was lying. Then they told me to look up. I still said,

"No."

I was giving the impression to leave me alone, but they would not leave. Then they told me,

"It will be okay, you are special."

They hugged me tightly. I didn't have the strength to hug them back. I was so upset. Seconds later I felt something different. I felt the sincerity in their hug. I broke down because love had defeated my pain. The love I had received strengthened me to hug the person back, and I thanked them with so much joy in my heart. Love prevailed and showed me its power, so I wanted all my relationships to be filled with love. You can't allow people to take your love away, because they will. You do not have to respond in the same way that hurt treats you. They say two wrongs don't make a right. Elder Milton once told me that "Love gives and lust takes." Get rid of all the lustful people in your life that want to take your happiness away from you. Find the loving people who want to encourage you and see you win in life.

I have had my ups and downs with relationships in my life, most of them being friendships. It is hard to find a good friend, so please when you do, hold on to them. Don't let your lustful ways damage a great thing. Sometimes we get caught up in our theory, and we forget to master it first. Relationships work both ways, so you have to live up to the example you wish to see as well. Stop evaluating other people. Sometimes before we do that, we must evaluate ourselves. The great ones self-assess. That's what we all need to do to help our relationships out. Don't be that person who convinces yourself that you're perfect. Learning is everlasting. So as you teach, please learn as well.

    The next thing you need to to look for when you are searching for meaningful relationships, is to find someone with goals. A person's goals will tell you everything you need to know about them. It will show whether you're compatible with them or not. If a person has goals, they are less likely to make mistakes. If you have goals, there is less time to dwell on the past because your concern is the future. You want someone in your life that you can have a future with. Goals will separate the average from the phenomenal. People only remember the phenomenal because they are the ones that last. People with goals will inspire you to set goals. You have to break out of your comfort zone and seek these people, because ultimately it takes you to the next level.

    Lastly, I can remember a time where I felt like I had no real relationships in my life. I questioned everyone but myself, only to find myself alone, left all by myself. One day I took a walk after midnight. I remember losing everything and just thinking about how to get back on my feet. At that moment I thought I had no one to turn to, so I turned to Jesus. He is my biggest relationship and through Him he provides all my needs. Everyone needs Jesus, because we all need to believe in something that is greater than us. God revealed to me my true identity. He accepted me when people denied me. His love was permanent, even when I didn't notice it. This whole time He has been protecting me.

    I am blessed to have my own relationship with God. I discovered that God wants us to come to Him. It doesn't matter how you decide to communicate with God, as long as you make

## Mindset

an effort. For such a long time I believed in religion, but religion just criticized me. There is no special way to get to know God, just position yourself. Some of us are trained to pray a certain way or say certain words, these things discouraged me. Eventually I had my own moment with God just walking by myself and opening up to God with all my heart. God doesn't give his heart in pieces, so neither should we.  As a father, you know that your son or daughter will make mistakes. A father's job is to protect and that's what God did for me. God reveals Himself to you based on your faith in Him. There are some important questions we should all ask ourselves, such as *how strong is my faith? Why is faith important?* When a person has faith in you, the level of your performance goes higher. Your sense of hope is filled with comfort in knowing that you can. Once I accepted Jesus as my Lord and Savior, my life headed in an upward direction. Every great relationship requires great sacrifice. You have to be willing to *give up*, so that your relationship can *go up*. Jesus made the greatest sacrifice for everyone; he died for our sins. That is something man can never fulfill.

    When I started my organization, I accepted anyone who wanted to be part of it. If you found interest in the mission, I felt like I couldn't tell you no. There were also a few people who I personally felt would be good additions to the team. Our team started out on fire! We were achieving our goals, and through adversity we worked together to overcame obstacles. I was able to be myself and learn about our organization's direction at the same time. I didn't have the most knowledge on what was going on, but I was committed to learn and grow for my team. I received a different vision every day, because I didn't work alone I worked with God. If it wasn't a different vision it was something that complimented the vision I already had. There is a season for

# Devantae Butler

everything. I am a firm believer in that saying, not only for things but for people. That's why when the direction of our group began to shift and people started to second guess the organization, I knew I had to elevate as a leader in order for us to elevate as an organization. One of the biggest problems I ran into was that some of my team members started to get too comfortable and became complacent. You cannot grow with someone who wants to stay where they are. My problem, personally, was that I wanted so badly to help them out. I tried to persuade them to come and be a part of what we were doing. I gave my heart to people who didn't want it, or who wouldn't do the same for me. This led me to a very stressful emotional state. I was hurting inside because I didn't know what to do or how to help. Then, because no action was taken, my condition only got worse. This decline impacted my group negatively, because I was the heart and soul. I knew something different had to happen. I was tired of expecting other people to get it done and I was tired of blaming them. In order to help myself, I began to blame me. I couldn't continue to expect others to change their perspective without changing my own first. I realized the hard way, that everyone doesn't want what you want. Therefore, they couldn't see what I saw. In order for me to strengthen my team, I had to let people go and strengthen myself. Once I did this I was able to see more clearly. I got the direction I needed. Then the right people either grew or fell into place.

    My team plays a very important role in my success today. I know that I cannot do everything by myself, but some of us try to convince ourselves that we don't need anyone. That's completely a lie. You must realize that everyone needs to have somebody, or else you will sink. Do not be so focused on others that you are blind to your own self. Once my focus shifted from people to

## Mindset

myself, the right people and things fell into place. Leadership starts at the top. When there's a problem with a team or company, it is a leadership problem first, not a player or employee. Sometimes we have to be the ones to choose the right relationships for our future, other times we don't choose at all, sometimes life just happens, and purpose is manifested. Continue to work on yourself, and your growth will spark others. People may depart from you during your process, but don't allow that to bother you.

**Devantae Butler**

## Chapter Fifteen: Be More

Our environment helps shape our tendencies, and it ultimately shapes our character. The environment I grew up in didn't help me because everyone had the same mindset and it was contagious in a bad way. Once I transferred schools and got a new perspective, I looked up to a lot of key people who were on the right track. Even though I looked up to them, they never really helped me or encouraged me to be great. It was like these people held in their wisdom to have a knowledge advantage over the next person. I was that kid who needed help but was afraid to show it, because it wasn't cool to ask for help. Life is all about perspectives, and I was developing the wrong one, so I made the decision to be different and help anyone I came across. I was not going to be selfish with information just because others were. I knew I had a story, and I had the aspiration to share it with the world. I wanted to speak to kids because I wanted to empower them to be great. I felt like people had held in information to themselves, and that's why our generation was falling apart.

As the Bible states, when people lack knowledge, they perish. There is no hope for the hopeless. I knew being honest and open would free my mind from old tendencies and help someone rise up. The first opportunity I had to speak to students was amazing. It was an immediate connection, and right there I knew that this was something I would do forever. I thought to myself, *if the people lack knowledge, and I have been given wisdom, then it is my responsibility to become a solution to their problem.* Become the thing you wish you had. That was my task. As I grew deeper in this direction, I discovered that it was a need. There are thousands of kids who feel the same way I felt. Have you ever told

## Mindset

yourself that what you're going through no one else would understand? Well, that's the mentality I had in my past, only to find out there are more people like me. I wanted to help people so that they did not suffer from the same things that I did. It brought peace to me knowing that no matter what I was going through, I could put a smile on someone else's face. It was amazing. So now, you can stop telling yourself *you can't*. We put limits on ourselves too much, when in reality we can do anything we set our minds to.

Be open-minded, that's true success. Shift your perspective from a "trying" state to an "I will" state. You must declare that great things can happen and don't worry about everything else. Believe that things will fall into place for you and they will. Be more than what you are exposed to. Records are meant to be broken; you must decide to fly before you take off. I went through so much and made so many mistakes along the way, that I could have told myself that advising kids was a bad idea. However, I realized that the mistakes were my advantage. We all want people in our lives that we can relate to. Therefore, I never speak to anyone with an attitude that I am better. I speak from a place that expresses how I can relate. No one is perfect, so do not judge people. There will always be someone faster, stronger, smarter, and more talented than you in life, but that doesn't mean anything other than you are human.

The best thing about you, is you. You must believe that first. When I started to believe in myself, I could no longer concern myself with previous thoughts or the opinion of others. I had to move forward with what was in my heart. I wanted to be the best, so I adopted the right attitude and I said *I'm going to train like the best*. Denzel Washington once said, "Hard work, works." You cannot be more if you continue to cheat and that was

## Devantae Butler

one of my biggest habits. The only person I was cheating was myself, because these same habits came back and hurt me. Just give your best so that you know how to get better. Just think about it like this, if you get better, then others will get better because of your example. Being more is all about having a positive outlook, coming from negative circumstances. It is a sense of hope that you can rise above what you are exposed to. There is someone inside of you that is stronger, wiser, and greater. Sometimes it's the challenges that life throws at us that help us to discover a more dominate person inside of us. Struggle breeds greatness. It is not easy to transform your life. It is not easy to separate yourself, but discipline is your friend. It is designed to help mold you into a better version of who you are now. Get up and take your walk. Write your story because I guarantee someone needs your voice, and your presence. Decide to become more and allow your actions to support your choices. I teach students seven steps that can be used to transform them into a greater version of self.

Number one is, face your fears. For such a long time, fear has held me back from seeing more in myself. Once I stepped outside my comfort zone, I discovered more about me. We all have our own personal fears that we must overcome. Number two is to have a plan/create a vision. This is important because we all have ideas which lead us to set goals, but we still need a vision for how we plan on following through. Number three is, have integrity. We must be honest with ourselves. There are too many situations that occur, where we do not tell ourselves the truth. We need morals, that way we cannot be influenced by anything that doesn't fit who we are. Number four is commit yourself. Ex-football star, Inky Johnson exemplifies this step very well. After suffering a career-ending injury that left him paralyzed in one

# Mindset

arm, Inky turned tragedy into triumph and became a notable motivational speaker. He expressed commitment to doing the very thing he said he was going to do, long after the mood or feeling had left him. He pushed on because he knew that someone was depending on his word, and in many cases your word is all you have. He uses his words to motivate others, rather than play the victim just because something bad happened to him. He committed. Number five is, believe. You must believe in yourself, even if others don't believe. Believing can change your current state. Number six is be positive. Positive thoughts will take your further in life than any car or airplane ever will. Number seven is be a leader. Leadership is a need that the world depends on. We need leaders to get results. The best thing anyone can do is discover that they are a leader in critical situations.

These seven components have helped me see life from a different outlook. These steps have become a part of me. In any situation that I face, these steps come to my mind. Some of them play bigger roles than the others. That's why you must instill important information in your heart, so that you can be it. I am not okay with just knowing what a great leader is; I won't be satisfied until I become a great leader. Knowing and having knowledge is only half the battle. It is what you do with what you know that leads to success. Understand this, people may not like you because your heart is set but they will acknowledge your results.

Stay the course and be persistent in all that you do and doors will open, but when you get into the door, you have to dominate. Bring everything you have into every day. Give everything and leave nothing. Limit your distractions and make no excuses, just produce. Once I became set on these ideas, my life went to the next level. I had discovered purpose. Amazing things

## Devantae Butler

will happen for you too once you become an everlasting learner; there's always something new to discover. Some of my greatest moments happened because I never settled. Maybe this was because I was searching for a better answer and outcome. Whatever the reason, I just believed that there was always more for me and all I had to do was keep God first.

Being more, for me, starts with the relationship I have with God. I didn't think I could make it to such a high level in life, and that's one reason I'm not there yet. As your faith increases, so does everything around you. People will be blessed because you have faith and you believe. Stay connected to Jesus because He will guide your footsteps. At times, we will doubt, and we will make poor choices, but God's love is unconditional. Therefore, when you're down and in a low place, when you feel like you can't do it, if you're worried about something, just know that God is getting ready to show up in your life.

You don't need everything in this life because the truth is that if you have Jesus, you do have everything. People say everything happens for a reason. Well self-reflect on the miracles that you have been exposed to. The signs in life are real; that gut feeling you have is real. The Bible says, "Greater is He that is within me than he that is in this world." This tells us that God is with you every day and with every step. Once I was more in my relationship with Him, my whole life changed in an amazing direction. I am humbled by what I have because the Bible teaches us that things can be taken away at any moment. When I decided to be more, I began embracing my family and friends. When I die, I want to be remembered as a person who did great things. I want to make a great impact for my generation. We all can do it but it starts with making a choice to be more. Surrender the bad habits about yourself. Surrender your pride, jealousy, and hatred. Give

# Mindset

love, hope, and effort moving forward in your life. Don't dwell on your past because it was an assessment for your future. Your future is what they will remember you for; it will one day become the past. Time is consistent and it stops for nothing and no one.

It's time to change your perspective and see what more your life can be. Once I decided this, I became my ultimate challenger. I embraced who I was becoming and the process. I understood that it would take time, so I should be patient with my process. Everyone has their own process on the path of greatness. The worst mistake you can make is viewing what someone else has, because it promotes envy. Be happy for others and bless as many people as you can and you will be blessed too. Give love and it will be given to you in the measure that it was received. Therefore, don't short yourself by being short with others. You will reap what you sow. Are you ready for your blessings? I never knew that all of this would happen in my life. I remember when I lost everything, I thought that things would never get better. I was so focused on what I could see that I couldn't see any further. I moved to a place where I stopped doubting and started claiming victory. Life is in the tongue. Speak it, and watch it come to pass. These things turned my mindset from nothing to something.

Life gives you very little to work with because all you have ever needed is inside. Search who you are for the truth, and the truth that was hidden in you all along. The truth is that you're special. Share who you are with the world because the world is waiting for you. Shift your perspective from how you view the world. The world needs your purpose, it needs your legacy. So, leave everything you can out there, and do not hold back your gifts. Never lose sight of why you started something and understand the importance of finishing. The one thing that is

## Devantae Butler

never an option is quitting. People have placed their faith in you. Recognize that the battle is bigger than you and continue to fight. Any transformation is going to be a fight, so stay strong in all that you do. Be ready to sacrifice time, people, and fun things. Everything has a price, especially growth. Take your personal growth *personally* and be determined. Become more intentional with your decisions, and don't be afraid to make mistakes. Failure leads to success and life is a risk. The mind is God's gift to you so do not waste it. Learn how to use it, and you can turn nothing into something. This is your life, so make sure to live it to your best potential. Tell yourself you can do all things through Christ who strengthens you. This is my mindset. What's yours?

# Mindset

## **Mindset Poem**

You are special, you are unique,
The scars of your past with help you achieve.
The impossible you were destined to be great.
I know it's hard to be patient but it is worth the wait.
Stop second guessing, you're called to shine bright.

You have been through too much not to continue and fight.
When you are feeling depressed remember this is your time.
There's no limit to the height in which you can fly.
When you think that you can't, decide to try.
You will be exposed to much more than the naked eye.

All you have to do is challenge yourself,
And ask tough questions like I need some help.
Be honest with who you are and the places you seek to go.
Say yes to your future and tell your past no.

I am so much more than what you thought I would be,
Once I decided to accept the real me.
Positive thoughts will take you a long way.
Take nothing for granted and conquer today.

What would a life be if I didn't have dreams?
Or having faith in something that I never believed?
It's time for you to rise up to the top of your mountain,
And give hope to all the people who doubted.
No matter what, give 100% in everything that you do,
And tell all along your journey that they can do it too.
It's a mindset.

# Devantae Butler

# **Tips to Shape Your Mindset**

- <u>Knowledge is Everywhere</u>
  A lot of people think that knowledge comes only in a school setting, but that's not true. Some of my favorite teachings in life came from the least expected moments. You can learn from anyone or anything.

- <u>Stay Healthy</u>
  My mom used to say to me, "Son, take care of your body now, and it will take care of you later."
  Your health is very important to your success.

- <u>High Energy is Key</u>
  Energy can be the difference between winning and losing, believe it or not. When you are energized you have enthusiasm and that is a great component to attack with. High-energy people get things done.

- <u>Set Goals</u>
  Goals are designed to hold you accountable so that you can achieve your mission. Set goals so high that you can't accomplish them until you grow into the person who can.

- <u>Ask Questions</u>
  Asking questions is powerful. It opens up so many doors besides the answers. Questions are a form of seeking, and wisdom is always around.

# Mindset

- <u>Be Persistent</u>
  Never stop, keep going no matter what. By continuing to knock, the door will open. Most people will give up. Just make sure you don't follow that bad example.

- <u>Be a Leader at all Times</u>
  Leadership is constant. There is no such thing as an on and off switch. Leaders are needed everywhere.

- <u>Speak Up</u>
  No one is going to speak up for your dreams the way you will. You have to use your voice, it's necessary.

- <u>Learn from all Mistakes</u>
  Mistakes will be made. You want to reduce yours by paying attention to the mistakes of others, so that you won't make the same ones.

- <u>Find People Who Appreciate your Worth</u>
  Do not allow other people to bring you down. Find people who will help you to grow.

- <u>Seek Purpose</u>
  Everything happens for a reason, so start to think why certain people are in your life, and why things are happening to you. You find what you are looking for.

- <u>Read the Bible</u>
  This is the book that will change your life for the better!

**Devantae Butler**

# 30 Day Inspiration Challenge:

God has given me wisdom. It has really helped me to better my mentality on how I receive things. Information is the key to opportunity. Here are 30 inspirational messages that will encourage you to take your life in a positive direction. Each message contains information of encouragement that came from my heart and ends with a scripture to support. I believe that faith is one of the most important traits to have, especially when pursing something that's bigger than you (such as your dreams). These messages are a reminder to never stop, a reminder on how purposed your life is. Go through these messages one day at a time for 30 days straight and watch how your days go to the next level, just by starting your day off on a positive note. Feed your spirit with great things early in the morning. Have you ever had a bad experience before class or work that you got upset, and then you told yourself *today's not going to be a good day*? Then you continue throughout your day and all you want is for the day to be over. Well that means that your focus is off. I realized that it is important to start your days off with positive things to avoid negative experiences. We have to protect our minds by staying focused on the positive energy instead of the negative energy. Take this information and let it take your mindset to the next level. (Read every message daily first thing in the morning.)

# Mindset

## **Morning Message Day 1:**

Everything is working in your favor. Many people will not understand why you take these steps. Continue to feed yourself with the word of the Lord, and ask and receive wisdom for true riches are in the understanding of his process and purpose for you. You can reach that next level and you will! Let's go have the best day ever, speak life into your situation.

***John 4:31-32:*** *Meanwhile his disciples urged him, "Rabbi eat something." But he said to them, "I have food to eat that you know nothing about."*

## **Morning Message Day 2:**

Today is your day, continue to be patient and blessed. Our Lord is all powerful and forgiving. He knows your needs, he sees your circumstances and He heard your prayers. Continue to be led by your faith and these things you ask for will begin to present themselves. Stay strong and hang in there. You are great. You are blessed. Have an amazing day!

***Ezekiel 12:25**: But I the Lord will speak what I will, and it shall be fulfilled without delay. For in your days, you rebellious people, I will fulfill whatever I say, declares the Sovereign Lord.*

# Mindset

## **Morning Message Day 3:**

You are a star and your light frightens the enemy! God is about to bring you into something powerful! Do not be discouraged by the things you are up against, instead embrace them with understanding. God has already brought you through! Now have a dominant day. Make someone smile today and the Lord will smile down at you!

***Isaiah 60:1-2*** *Arise, shine, for your light has come, and the glory of the Lord rises upon you. See, darkness covers the earth and thick darkness is over the peoples, but the Lord rises upon you and his glory appears over you.*

## **Morning Message Day 4:**

God is making a way for you already! Stand firm right now and continue to press towards goodness and love! This is your month, claim it! Your new joy is coming. The better you, will present itself in this month. Stay focused and go after your dreams and aspirations. This is your time and moment. You are built to last, so carry on with a phenomenal day!

***Jeremiah 31:3-4**: The Lord appeared to us in the past, saying: "I have loved you with an everlasting love; I have drawn you with unfailing kindness. I will build you up again, and you, Virgin Israel, will be rebuilt. Again you will take up your timbrels and go out to dance with the joyful."*

# Mindset

## **Morning Message Day 5:**

Today will be victorious for you. God sees and knows your heart! You no longer have to fight these battles alone. Continue to challenge yourself and do the things necessary to get to that next level of your life. For every next level of your life demands a different version of you. Inky Johnson says, "Step into that today. God will hold your hand through it all, so be blessed and be encouraged."

***1 Corinthians 15:57-58**: But thanks be to God! He gives us the victory through our Lord Jesus Christ. Therefore, my dear brothers and sisters, stand firm. Let nothing move you. Always give yourselves fully to the work of the Lord, because you know that your labor in the Lord is not in vain.*

## Morning Message Day 6:

Let's refocus on the things that matter. It's okay to get distracted. We all do, but now is the time to say *no more* and regain your focus on your goals and assignments! There's no limit to what you can do. Stop holding you back! It's time right now, to take pride in your next decision to get things done vs. waste time. It's time to rise up and grind.

*Jeremiah 29:11*: "For I know the plans I have for you," declares the Lord, "plans to prosper you and not to harm you, plans to give you hope and a future."

# Mindset

**Morning Message Day 7:**
In many cases, people will be in disagreement with you because they don't understand how strong your faith is toward something. Do not let anyone knock you off of your roots which you have planted and have now become a part of who you are. All adversity isn't bad. It can be used as that tool that strengthens your character and it is necessary for the direction you are headed. Be blessed and keep going no matter what. Believe!

***Job 2:10****: He replied, "You are talking like a foolish woman. Shall we accept good from God, and not trouble?" In all this, Job did not sin in what he said.*

## Morning Message Day 8:

It's time. You are special. Do not let things that you cannot control, affect anything about you. Continue to love and express who you are, despite your difficulties. The Lord has held your hand and has been with you. He has never turned on you, even when you turned on Him. Grace has kept you, so be joyful for today is the day you walk in favor. You have been chosen for such a time as this. So rise up!

**Roman 12:2**: *Do not conform to the pattern of this world, but be transformed by renewing of your mind. Then you will be able to test and approve what God's will is—His good, pleasing and perfect will.*

# Mindset

**Morning Message Day 9:**
What is the purpose of a sports playbook? It possesses the play call and the mindset of the coach. It's important to know the playbook because there may be times in life ,when you cannot huddle up, and you have to have the knowledge about what's going on and take action! Well God is saying "here's my playbook, here's my word." Those who know it and use it can never lose, because the Lord's word is true! Use the word as a weapon. Information is powerful, so we have to tap into the tools that are given to us.

*Matthew 7:24-25: Therefore everyone who hears these words of mine and puts them into practice is like a wise man who built his house on rock. The rain came down, the streams rose, and the winds blew and beat against that house; yet it did not fall, because it had its foundation on the rock.*

## **Morning Message Day 10:**

Pay attention to the things in front of you, for there's always a message that God wants to show you. Only the people who have the desire to seek will find the purpose in every teaching. Open yourself up in order to understand what others will fail to recognize. By releasing things inside, you give yourself the advantage to respond to the truth. You are great, keep going!

**Proverbs 5:1-2**: *My son, pay attention to my wisdom, turn your ear to my words of insight, that you may maintain discretion and your lips may preserve knowledge.*

# Mindset

## **Morning Message Day 11:**

Now is the time for you. Remain focused for you are valuable. Your gift is unique and your heart is full of love. God honors the righteous, so do not allow negative thoughts to consume your mind. The enemy plans on intimidating you because he cannot touch you. God is fighting for you, so step out in faith and believe in who God has called you to be. Nothing can stop you, so be great!

*Joshua 1:9: Have I not commanded you? Be strong and courageous. Do not be afraid; do not be discouraged, for the Lord your God will be with you wherever you go.*

## **Morning Message Day 12:**

The way you fight darkness is with light. So don't allow negativity to change your mood. Keep fighting with love and kindness. I know it's hard, but this will leave a stamp on people who do not know what change can do. Be the change you want to see, because you have the ability to do it. You are unique and wonderfully made.

***1 Corinthians 13:4-8**: Love is patient, love is kind. It does not envy, it does boast, it is not proud. It does not dishonor others, it is not self-seeking, it is not easily angered, it keeps no record of wrongs. Love does not delight in evil but rejoices with the truth. It always protects, always trusts, always hopes, always perseveres. Love never fails. But where there are prophecies, they will cease; where there are tongues, they will be stilled; where there is knowledge, it will pass away.*

# Mindset

## Morning Message Day 13:

When love and truth are in your heart, you enable their access to become the difference in many lives. Do not idolize self, for that is unlike God. Give with good intentions and be joyful in what you give, without expectations of collateral. God will honor your good deeds and He sees your heart.

**James 4:3** *When you ask, you do not receive, because you ask with wrong motives, that you may spend what you get on your pleasures.*

## **Morning Message Day 14:**

Faith will carry you over the hump into victory. You will unlock many doors by keeping your faith in the Lord. Do not look at your problems to break you. God is using them to boost you! Allow God's blessings to pour down on you, for your faith will bring you through the impossible.

***1 Peter 1:5-7**: Who through faith are shielded by Gods power until the coming of salvation that is ready to be revealed in the last time. In all this you greatly rejoice, though now for a little while you may have had to suffer grief in all kinds of trials. These have come so that the proven genuineness of your faith—of greater worth than gold, which perishes even though refined by fire—may result in praise, glory and honor when Jesus Christ is revealed.*

# Mindset

## **Morning Message Day 15:**

Find peace and joy in your faith in the Lord. The enemy is trying to hold back your gifting from the world by attacking your mentality, hoping doubt will be in your head. However, for every attack the enemy carries out, God has a counter to bring you up stronger in any situation. God will make you bigger! Keep pressing to reach greater.

***Psalms 23:3-4:*** *He refreshes my soul. He guides me along the right paths for his name's sake. Even though I walk through the darkest valley, I will fear no evil, for you are with me; your rod and your staff, they comfort me.*

## **Morning Message Day 16:**

The choices you make are a result of your character. How do you want to be remembered, and what is the foundation you have to ask yourself? Many people will shy away from what's in their heart because they are too concerned about the opinions of others. Do not be afraid to be yourself and don't allow yourself to convince you that you're somebody you're not.

*Galatians 5:13: You, my brothers and sisters, were called to be free. But do not use your freedom to indulge the flesh; rather, serve one another humbly in love.*

## Mindset

**Morning Message Day 17:**
Every moment is critical because it has a teaching that will help your growth. Do not get upset about your lonely moments because isolation is critical for your development. No one is going to understand your process, because they don't know the many battles (mentally) you have already overcome. So continue to grow, and just know the Lord is proud of you! I pray you have a great and blessed day! Embrace your process.

*Psalms 121:7-8: The Lord will keep you from all harm—he will watch over your life; the Lord will watch over your coming and going both now and forevermore.*

## **Morning Message Day 18:**

Begin to recognize the purpose in every moment, seek it out. This is your time for growth. Every season is a different learning process to enhance who you are. Embrace every moment because there's no time to miss opportunities. It's better to be prepared and not have an opportunity, than to have an opportunity and not be prepared. Take advantage and have a blessed day.

***Ecclesiastes 3:1****: There is a time for everything, and a season for every activity under the heavens.*

## Mindset

### Morning Message Day 19:

Your calling and purpose mean that you will have to alter relationships with people. It's not that they are different from you, but because of who you are becoming, many people will no longer be in a parallel position with you. Do not shun the new lessons from new people in your life. You do not want to miss your blessings due to lack of understanding on your part. Embrace information, for knowledge is power! You're powerful too, so walk in purpose and be blessed!

***Isaiah 43:18-19**: Forget the former things; do not dwell on the past. See, I am doing a new thing! Now it springs up; do you not perceive it? I am making a way in the wilderness and streams in the wasteland.*

## **Morning Message Day 20:**

That supernatural area of your life requires a certain type of belief on your part. Your dream, goals, and desires are possible if you are led by your faith. Believe that supernatural things will happen for you, despite your hard times and what others think. Be led by your faith and remember there's a blessing in the storm that you are in, so keep going. Your breakthrough is near!

***James 2:17-18***: *In the same way, faith by itself, if it is not accompanied by action, is dead. But someone will say, "You have faith; I have deeds." Show me your faith without deeds, and I will show you my faith by my deeds.*

# Mindset

## Morning Message Day 21:
Every obstacle has great purpose behind it. How can you pass a test without knowledge of the information? Resources and wisdom have been given to you to get past your next obstacle or test. Good things come to those who believe, better things come to those who are patient, and the best things comes to those who DON'T QUIT. Today is your day. Raise your bar! Getting to the next level of your life is critical, not just for you but the people depending on you. Rise up!

**James 1:12**: *Blessed is the one who perseveres under trial because, having stood the test, that person will receive the crown of life that the Lord has promised to those who love him.*

## **Morning Message Day 22:**

Be fearless and be bold for the things you stand for. Strengthen your foundation by increasing your faith and demanding your very best. Nothing can hold you back but you, so stop holding you back. Today, say "no more" and begin to climb your mountain and reach your top!

**Deuteronomy 31:6**: Be strong and courageous. Do not be afraid or terrified because of them, for the Lord your God goes with you; he will never leave you nor forsake you.

# Mindset

## **Morning Message Day 23:**

Today take control of your life. Begin to be healed by being open to your weaknesses. Love others as you love yourself. Treat people how want to be treated. Your breakthrough is vital for someone else who needs your testimony to get through. Don't ignore the information you have in front of you. Be healed today and be better. You are forgiven and you are needed, so be open and be blessed.

***Ephesians 4:31-32****: Get rid of all bitterness, rage and anger, brawling and slander, along with every form of malice. Be kind and compassionate to one another, forgiving each other, just as in Christ God forgave you.*

## Morning Message Day 24:

Do not be quick to judge, instead be eager to learn and be patient with others. You can have a greater impact by adjusting and becoming the example we are trying to express. Speak light into the life of others. Pray for people, because there is power in prayer. You have the key to get rid of darkness, and you can change the atmosphere.

***James 5:16**: Therefore confess your sins to each other and pray for each other so that you may be healed. The prayer of righteous person is powerful and effective.*

## Mindset

**Morning Message Day 25:**
You are blessed. Never take what you have for granted. Humble yourself because there was once a point in time when you didn't have. Begin to appreciate, greatly, everything around you! Give thanks and share with others the good news as a sign and reminder that they are blessed too! Have an awesome day.

*__Jonah 2:6-7__: To roots of the mountains I sank down; the earth beneath barred me in forever. But you, Lord my God, brought my life up from the pit. When my life was ebbing away, I remembered you, Lord, and my prayer rose to you, to your holy temple.*

## Morning Message Day 26:

Mistakes will be made, adversity is bound to occur. Do not overwhelm yourself, for the Lord loves his son Jesus. He just expects more from you because you are blessed and highly favored. Never put in your mind that you cannot come to him. He is waiting on you! He loves you! Every mistake is one step closer to success. Do not let hard times leave you weary, instead be cheerful because a new level of knowledge is coming.

*Joel 2:13*: *Rend your hearts and not your garments. Return to the Lord your God, for he is gracious and compassionate, slow to anger and abounding in love, and be relents from sending calamity.*

# Mindset

## **Morning Message Day 27:**
In order to gain more, you must seek more. You are looking at situations from the wrong point of view. Adjust your vision to see what the enemy is trying to hide from you in the shadow. Now is your time! Be filled by your purpose and who God has called you to be. Be more!

***1 Samuel 2:4-5****: The bows of the warriors are broken, but those who stumbled are armed with strength. Those who were full hire themselves out for food, but those who were hungry are hungry no more. She who was barren has borne seven children, but she who has had many sons pines away.*

## Morning Message Day 28:

Don't look at the wrong in your life or in your situation. Understand that everything is happening in your favor. God wants to turn your bad into good, he wants our praise. He plans to give you a new vision to be able to look at your situation differently! He is a wonderful God. He's calling for you to take his hand so you can receive his blessing.

*Habakkuk 3:17-18*: *Though the fig tree does not bud and there are no grapes on the vines, though the olive crop fails and the fields produce no food, though there are no sheep in the pen and no cattle in the stalls, yet I will rejoice in the Lord. I will be joyful in God my savior.*

# Mindset

## **Morning Message Day 29:**

Anytime you engage in something new, find something new to get out of it, something that cannot be physically given to you, and use it as a motive to keep your interest. You have to establish more to receive more. Create the basis of your foundation on good things, that way when bad things occur you will not be moved. Stay true to the mission. Have a great day.

**Mark 4:17**: *But since they have no root, they last only a short time. When trouble or persecution comes because of the word, they quickly fall away.*

## **Morning Message Day 30:**

This is a big time for you. Allow nothing to stop you from pressing forward! Sometimes you have to go through darkness to get to the light. Your light is already prepared for you. No matter what, continue to keep walking. There is light at the end, so get ready to receive a blessing you have never received before. It's your time these, and are your moments.

***Revelation 7:16-17****: Never again will they hunger; never again will they thirst. The sun will not beat down on them, nor any scorching heat. For the Lamb at the center of the throne will be their shepherd; he will lead them to springs of living waters. And God will wipe every tear from their eyes.*

# Mindset

# ABOUT THE AUTHOR

My name is Devantae Butler. I am 24 years old and a man of God. I'm very excited to have the opportunity to share my perspective on what I believe shapes a great mindset. Born on May 15, 1993, I was what I believed to be a regular kid. I grew up in Pittsburgh, Pennsylvania. I loved the game of football. It was what I did and who I was, a football player. School was a challenge for me only because I never took it seriously. I attended Gateway School District for the majority of my education. I graduated high school in 2012 and attended Community College of Allegheny County. Not taking school seriously, I was placed on academic probation within my first two years and lost my financial aid. This hardship forced me to work two jobs to purchase my first car at the age of 20.

My attitude was terrible at this point in my life and I believed that the world revolved around me. I recall a time when I came home and I questioned my little brother about where his homework was and he responded saying,

> "You're not even in school! So, don't tell me to do my homework."

This stuck with me and caused me to look myself in the mirror and begin to hold myself accountable. Days later, I got into a big argument with my parents and stormed out of the house. I was asked by a group of friends the next day to drive them to a university to see some friends. I agreed and that was a turning point in my life. My brother and I (along with the three other passengers) were involved in a car accident the night of February 9, 2014. We hit a guard rail going down the parkway and I was ejected from the vehicle breaking my ribs, piecing my lungs, and fracturing my ankle. Everyone survived the accident, but I could barely move my body. I remember asking my brother what happened while we were in the hospital. He was the only one out

## Devantae Butler

of all five of us who had no injuries and he said,

"Bro I prayed."

That moment really opened my eyes. I was unable to walk for two months and had a lot of time to think. My family showed me more love and support than I felt that I deserved. While lying in bed my mindset started to change.

I started to view the situation as a second chance at life. Things would be different now. Every decision made from here on out would serve a purpose. Using my little brother's words as motivation to press forward, I promised myself to get readmitted into school. I also created a non-profit organization known as *Reaching New Dreams & Recognizing Talents*. I wanted to inspire others to reach for new dreams, which requires doing something outside of their comfort zones, and ultimately lead them to the recognition of their own talents within. I have fully committed to what I feel is my purpose in life, inspiring others to be transparent and not allowing anything to stop my pursuit to climb the ladder of my full potential. I have discovered the greatness inside of me by challenging myself in uncomfortable moments. Our organization focuses on youth event planning, mentoring, motivational speaking engagements, and more. I made a decision to chase after personal growth and not make excuses for why I'm in the situation I placed myself in. I hope this book gives you momentum to achieve what others didn't envision you doing. You have a gift but as my mentor once said,

"What good is a gift if you don't give it away?"

Ladies and gentlemen, it starts with your MINDSET!

www.ingramcontent.com/pod-product-compliance
Lightning Source LLC
Chambersburg PA
CBHW051946160426
43198CB00013B/2324